John R. Sweney, L. L. Pickett, William J. Kirkpatrick

Cheerful Songs

John R. Sweney, L. L. Pickett, William J. Kirkpatrick

Cheerful Songs

ISBN/EAN: 9783337180928

Printed in Europe, USA, Canada, Australia, Japan

Cover: Foto ©Thomas Meinert / pixelio.de

More available books at **www.hansebooks.com**

CHEERFUL SONGS.

BY
WILLIAM J. KIRKPATRICK,
JOHN R. SWENEY, AND L. L. PICKETT.

LOUISVILLE, KY.:
PICKETT PUBLISHING COMPANY,
165 FOURTH AVENUE.

PREFACE.

THERE are many books of song in the market, but the editors of this work humbly trust that it has a mission in the world. They send it out with the prayer that many souls may be helped on toward the blessed Land of Song by it.

CHEERFUL SONGS.

3 GLORY TO THE LAMB.

1 Come let us join our cheerful songs
  With angels round the throne,
Ten thousand thousand are their
  tongues,
  But all their joys are one.

Chorus.

Glory to the Lamb!
Glory to the Lamb!
Glory to the Lamb of God.
Glory to the Lamb!
Glory to the Lamb!
Glory to the Lamb of God.

2 "Worthy the Lamb that died," they
  cry,
  "To be exalted thus!"
"Worthy the Lamb!" our hearts reply,
  "For he was slain for us."

3 Jesus is worthy to receive
  Honor and pow'r divine;
And blessings more than we can give,
  Be, Lord, forever thine.

4 The whole creation join in one,
  To bless the sacred name
Of him that sits upon the throne,
  And to adore the Lamb.
                          Isaac Watts.

3

4 THE FOUNTAIN FROM THE ROCK.

1 I HAVE come to the fountain that flows
    from the Rock,
  The Rock that was smitten for me;
  For I heard a sweet voice gently speak
    to my soul:
  "O come to the waters so free."

Chorus.

O wonderful fountain that flows from
    the Rock,
  What tides of salvation outpour!
'Tis for you, 'tis for me, hallelujah!
Take freely, and thirst nevermore.

2 While I drink of the fountain that flows
    from the Rock,
  Sweet peace, like a beautiful dove,
  Nestles down in my heart, while the
    Spirit divine,
  Awakens the music of love.

3 There is strength at the fountain that
    flows from the Rock,
  For life everlasting is there;
  And the soul gains a power that will
    victory win,
  In hours of temptation and care.

4 I'll abide by the fountain that flows
    from the Rock,
  And sink 'neath its bright, cleansing
    waves;
  All its waters are sparkling with heav-
    enly light;
  Our Jesus abundantly saves.

                          E. E. Hewitt.

5 HIM THAT COMETH UNTO ME.

1 LISTEN to the blessèd invitation,
    Sweeter than the notes of angel-song,
Chiming softly with a heavenly cadence,
    Calling to the passing throng.

Chorus.

Him that cometh unto me,
Him that cometh unto me,
Him that cometh unto me,
    I will in nowise cast out.

2 Weary toiler, sad and heavy-laden,
    Joyfully the great salvation see,
Close beside thee stands the Burden-
    bearer,
    Strong to bear thy load and thee.

3 Come, ye thirsty, to the living waters,
    Hungry, come and on his bounty feed,
Not thy fitness is the plea to bring him,
    But thy pressing, utmost need.

4 "Him that cometh," blind or maimed
    or sinful,
    Cometh for his healing touch divine,
For the cleansing of the blood so pre-
    cious,
    Prove anew this gracious line.

5 Coming humbly, daily to this Saviour,
    Breathing all the heart to him in
    prayer;
Coming some day to the heavenly man-
    sions,
    He will give thee welcome there.
                   E. E. Hewitt.

6 REVIVE THE HEARTS OF ALL.

1 God is here, and that to bless us
    With the Spirit's quick'ning power;
See, the cloud already bending,
    Waits to drop the grateful shower.

Chorus.

Let it come, O Lord, we pray thee,
    Let the shower of blessing fall;
We are waiting, we are waiting,
    O revive the hearts of all.

2 God is here! we feel his presence
    In this consecrated place;
But we need the soul-refreshing
    Of his free, unbounded grace.

3 God is here! O then, believing,
    Bring to him our one desire,
That his love may now be kindled,
    Till its flame each heart inspire.

4 Saviour, grant the prayer we offer,
    While in simple faith we bow,
From the windows of thy mercy
    Pour us out a blessing now.
                James L. Black.

7   HOW ARE YOU LIVING?

1 How, O how are you living, my brother?
    Are you going the pilgrimage way?
Are you doing the will of your Master?
    Are you living for Jesus to-day?

Refrain.

Are you living for Jesus to-day, to-day?
Are you living for Jesus to-day?
 O tell me, my friend and my brother,
Are you living for Jesus to-day?

2 Earth will offer you pleasures, my
    brother,
   Have you turned from these pleasures
     away?
 Are you striving to work for the Master?
 Are you living for Jesus to-day?

3 Sin will surely entice you, my brother,
   Quickly turn from temptation away;
 O then give all your life to the Master,
 And be living for Jesus to-day.

4 You may grow cold and careless, my
    brother,
   And from Christ and his following
     stray;
 Are you watching and praying and
    trusting?
 Are you living for Jesus to-day?
                              Rev. E. A. Hoffman.

8   Trusting in the Name of Jesus.

1 In perfect peace I now can say,
   Trusting in the name of Jesus,
 I walk with God from day to day,
   Trusting in the name of Jesus;
 I walk by faith and not by sight,
   Trusting in the name of Jesus,
 His love my theme from morn till night,
   Trusting in the name of Jesus.

7

Chorus.

Trusting in the name of Jesus,
Only in the name of Jesus,
I walk with God from day to day,
Trusting in the name of Jesus.

2 I came with guilt and sin oppressed,
Trusting in the name of Jesus,
I took his yoke and found sweet rest,
Trusting in the name of Jesus;
How light my burdens now appear,
Trusting in the name of Jesus!
I have no time for doubt or fear,
Trusting in the name of Jesus.

3 Beneath the hallowed mercy-seat,
Trusting in the name of Jesus,
I sit enraptured at his feet,
Trusting in the name of Jesus;
And when my span of life is o'er,
Trusting in the name of Jesus,
My soul shall fly to yonder shore,
Trusting in the name of Jesus.

Carrie M. Wilson.

9 DEAR SAVIOUR, CLEANSE ME NOW.

1 A TREMBLING soul I come to thee,
And, if there yet is room for me
In yonder fount so full and free,
Dear Saviour, cleanse me now.

Chorus.

Cleanse me now, cleanse me now,
Blessèd Saviour, cleanse me now;
A trembling soul I come to thee,
Dear Saviour, cleanse me now.

8

2 I come in simple faith alone,
  To plead thy merits—not my own;
  I lay my heart before thy throne,
    Dear Saviour, cleanse me now.

3 I long to feel thy pow'r divine,
  To see thy light around me shine,
  And know henceforth that I am thine,
    Dear Saviour, cleanse me now.

4 My life and breath, my heart and soul,
  I gladly yield to thy control;
  O let the healing waters roll,
    Dear Saviour, cleanse me now.
                              Frank Gould.

10   SEND ME.

1 ARE there those around my door,
    Whom I thoughtless do not see,
  Sick, neglected, wretched, poor,
    From their sin and suff'ring sore?
    Here am I, O Lord, send me.

              Chorus.
    Send me, send me;
  Here am I, O Lord, send me,
    Send me, send me;
  Here am I, O Lord, send me.

2 Are there those who're far from home,
    Far from home, O Lord, and thee?
  O'er the wilds who lawless roam,
    'Neath the white Sierras' dome?
    Here am I, O Lord, send me.

3 Are there those who wretched hide,
    Sunk in sin to low degree,
On some city's surging tide,
    Lost to love and truth and pride?
    Here am I, O Lord, send me.

4 Are there those who know thee not,
    On some island of the sea?
In some lone, neglected spot,
    Stained by many a sin and blot?
    Here am I, O Lord, send me,

5 Send me where thou knowest best,
    Where the greatest need may be;
Where men are the most unblest,
    Tossed upon their sin's unrest.
    Here am I, O Lord, send me.

Rev. J. E. Rankin, D.D.

11   GOOD NEWS.

1 GOOD news! good news of a soul re-
    deemed,
    A penitent forgiven!
Good news! good news that another
    friend
    Is on the way to heaven!

Chorus.

Rejoice! rejoice! there's joy to-day
    In the land beyond the river;
Another gem for His diadem,
    A star to shine forever.

2 Good news! good news that another
    heart
    Has learned redemption's story;

Good news! good news that another
  voice
Will sing his praise in glory.

3 Good news! good news that another life
  Will show the power of Jesus,
Will prove the might of the saving grace
Which daily, hourly frees us.

4 Good news! good news that another
  hand
  Will precious seed be sowing,
Another guide to lead straying feet
Where living streams are flowing.
E. E. Hewitt.

12 RESTING BY AND BY!

1 CHRISTIANS are you growing weary?
  There'll be resting by and by;
Is your pathway dark and dreary?
  There'll be resting by and by.

Refrain.

There'll be resting by and by,
There'll be resting by and by,
When the toils of life are over,
There'll be resting by and by.

2 Have you many hours of anguish?
  There'll be resting by and by,
Where your soul will no more languish;
  There'll be resting by and by.

3 Cheer up, then, no longer fearing,
  There'll be resting by and by;
When you see our Lord's appearing,
  There'll be resting by and by.

11

4 Let us work, and keep on praying,
  There'll be resting by and by;
  If we come his word obeying?
  There'll be resting by and by.

Rev W. E. Penn.

13

THEN REJOICE, ALL YE RANSOMED.

1 THERE's rejoicing in the presence of the
    angels
  Over sinners coming home,
  All the heav'nly harpers, with a mighty
    chorus,
  Now are praising round the throne.

Chorus.

Then rejoice, all ye ransomed,
  Let your praises reach to heaven's
    highest dome;
For the dead's alive, the lost is found,
    and
Wand'rers now are coming, coming
  home.

2 O how happy is the sinner who has
    tasted
  Of the Saviour's wondrous love,
  Love that bringeth peace and joy, which
    passeth knowledge,
  Ever given from above.

3 In the home where once was strife and
    pain and sorrow,
  There'll be blessèd peace and joy,

12

Prayer and praise to God around the
 family altar
Will the power of sin destroy.

4 We will rally 'round the standard of our
 Saviour,
 And to others loudly call:
"Come, ye sinners, and repent, believe
 in Jesus:
 He will freely pardon all."

E. F. Miller.

14   FOLLOW ME.

1 HEAR you not the Saviour calling,
 Calling you so earnestly?
Gently, too, the tones are falling:
 "Come, O come, and follow me."

Chorus.

Let us round our Leader rally,
 Jesus bids us each to come;
He will lead us through the valley,
 O'er the river, safely home.

2 Lay not up on earth your treasure,
 Transient, perishing 'twill be;
Rather seek eternal pleasure;
 Would you find it, follow me.

3 In my Father's house in heaven,
 Let your hearts untroubled be,
Glorious mansion will be given,
 Only come and follow me.

4 Be thy pathway bright or dreary
 Whither duty leadeth thee,

13

Strong thy steps, or faint and weary,
I will guide thee: follow me.

5 When thy days on earth are ending,
And the close of life you see,
Even to the grave descending,
Never fear, but follow me.

T. C. O'Kane.

15 GATHER THEM IN.

1 GATHER them in at the Master's call
To the banquet of his love;
Go bring them in, there's room for all
In the Father's house above.

Chorus.

Go, then, and tell them, go and compel
them;
Gather them out of the mire of sin;
Go, then, and tell them, go and compel
them,
Gather them in, O gather them in!

2 Gather them in, the halt and lame,
By the winning word and deed;
There is healing still in the wondrous
name,
And a help for ev'ry need.

3 Gather them in, there's none so low
But the Lord shall bid him "Rise;"
There is none so sunk in the deeps of woe
But may climb the highest skies!

4 Gather them in, the young and old,
For the Father's love is free;

14

For each and all there's a harp of gold,
 And a house by the jasper sea.

5 Then as the blood-washed raise their
  songs
  To the Lamb upon the throne,
 As you hear the harps of the countless
  throngs
 Their joy will swell your own.
Rev. Henry Burton, M.A.

16   ALL BRIGHT ABOVE.

1. I SEE the bright, effulgent rays
  Outbeaming from the Saviour's face;
 No dark'ning clouds obscure the sight
  Of his sweet smile—my life, my light.

Refrain.

 I am mounting on wings, I am soaring
  on high,
  Where the sun's ever shining in un-
  clouded sky,
 In the joy of his presence, the smiles of
  his love;
  O glory to Jesus! 'tis all bright above;
 'Tis all bright above, 'tis all bright above,
  O glory to Jesus, 'tis all bright above!

2 O blessèd vision! glad surprise!
  It breaks upon my wand'ring eyes—
 The Sun of righteousness divine,
  In whom the Father's glories shine.

3 Triumphant Christ! all conqu'ring King!
  Thy praises I delight to sing;
 Thy glory shines around me here,
  My path is bright, my sky is clear.
Mrs. Mary D. Jones.

17 ACCORDING TO YOUR FAITH.

1 BLEST Saviour, what a word is this!
My heart leaps as I read;
'Tis all the strength, the love, the bliss
We weary sinners need.

Refrain.

"According to your faith"
Is what the Saviour saith;
Lord, I believe,
And now receive
According to my faith.

2 It claims our Father's boundless store,
The riches of his grace,
Greater than angel's thought, and more
Than angel's hand can trace.

3 Pardon and peace and holiness,
And heaven's own reward—
Saviour, astonished, we confess
Never was such a word.

4 All, all is ours by simple faith,
Nothing have we to do,
But rest on what the Saviour saith,
And find his word is true.

Rev. J. L. Stokes.

18 BEAUTIFUL DAY.

1 BEAUTIFUL day, lovely thy light;
Holy each ray, banishing night;
Cloudless thy sky; peaceful my stay
Here in the sunlight of beautiful day.

Refrain.

Beautiful, beautiful day,
Evermore shine on my way;
Saviour, I pray, keep me alway
Safe in this beautiful day.

2 Beautiful day, calm was thy dawn;
Joyous the lay, blessèd the morn,
When in my heart, over my way,
First shone the noontide of beautiful
day.

3 Beautiful day, perfectly bright;
Jesus alway, boundless delight,
Bliss all around, heav'n by the way,
Shining in fullness, O beautiful day!

4 Beautiful day, haven of rest;
Ev'ry one may come and be blest;
Glory to God! naught can dismay;
Christ is the light of this beautiful day.

19   WHAT A WONDERFUL SAVIOUR!

1 CHRIST has for sin atonement made,
   What a wonderful Saviour!
We are redeemed, the price is paid,
   What a wonderful Saviour!

Refrain.

What a wonderful Saviour is Jesus,
   my Jesus!
What a wonderful Saviour is Jesus,
   my Lord!

2 I praise him for the cleansing blood,
   What a wonderful Saviour!

That reconciled my soul to God;
What a wonderful Saviour!

3 He cleansed my heart from all its
sins,
What a wonderful Saviour!
And now he reigns and rules therein,
What a wonderful Saviour!

4 He walks beside me in the way,
What a wonderful Saviour!
And keeps me faithful day by day,
What a wonderful Saviour!

5 He gives me overcoming power,
What a wonderful Saviour!
And triumph in each conflict hour,
What a wonderful Saviour!

6 To him I've given all my heart,
What a wonderful Saviour!
The world shall never share a part,
What a wonderful Saviour!

E. A. Hoffman.

20   I Want to Be a Worker.

1 I want to be a worker for the Lord,
I want to love and trust his holy word;
I want to sing and pray, and be busy
every day
In the vineyard of the Lord.

Chorus.

I will work, I will pray,
In the vineyard, in the vineyard of the
Lord;

I will work, I will pray,
I will labor every day
In the vineyard of the Lord.

2 I want to be a worker ev'ry day,
I want to lead the erring in the way
That leads to heaven above, where all
    is peace and love
In the kingdom of the Lord.

3 I want to be a worker strong and brave,
I want to trust in Jesus' power to save;
All who will truly come shall find a
    happy home
In the kingdom of the Lord.

4 I want to be a worker; help me, Lord,
To lead the lost and erring to thy word,
That points to joy on high, where pleas-
    ures never die
In the kingdom of the Lord.

I. Baltzell.

21   WHATSOEVER.

1 WHATSOEVER, in my name
Ask, and thou receiv'st the same;
Whatsoever thou dost require,
Faith in Christ gains thy desire.

Chorus.

In the Saviour's precious name
    All our prayers shall offered be,
And his grace shall answer give,
    If our faith but bring the plea.

2 Is thy heart bowed down with sin?
Jesus longs to enter in;
Longs to take thy load away,
Longs to purge thy soul to-day.

3 Hast thou wandered from thy God,
And deserv'st his chast'ning rod?
Go to him on bended knee;
Ask in faith, he'll pardon thee.

4 Is thy soul with sorrow riv'n?
And in vain with it hast striv'n?
Carry all to God in prayer;
Thou shalt be of heav'n an heir.

5 Is thy life with care oppressed?
Liv'st thou even in distress?
Jesus Christ, the Man of grief,
Gives, to all who seek, relief.

6 Wilt thou by his hand be led?
And by waters still be fed,
Drinking draughts of grace divine?
Live then always in the Vine.

7 May our trust from day to day
Gleam, O Lord, with brightest ray,
Till we see thee face to face,
Perfect in thy pow'r and grace.

J. A. Holland.

22   COME HOME.

1 THE Saviour invites you, poor wan-
d'rer, to come,
The Father is waiting to welcome you
home;

Now cease from your wand'rings so
lonely and wild;
Return to your Father, O prodigal
child!

Chorus.

Come home, come home,
O prodigal child, come home!

2 Return to the Father who holds you
so dear;
Say, why will you perish when plenty
is near?
O leave the lone desert where shadows
are piled;
Return to your Father, O prodigal
child!

3 Poor wanderer, haste, for the night
draweth nigh;
Say, why will you linger still? Why
will you die?
Though poor and unworthy, with sin
all defiled;
The Father will welcome his prodigal
child!

4 Come home, trembling mourner, O
come and be blest,
Here lay down your burdens that you
may find rest;
Be cleansed from your sins, and to God
reconciled;
Return to your Father, O prodigal
child!

W. F. Cosner.

23 TRUSTING ONLY THEE.

1 I am trusting thee, Lord Jesus,
    Trusting only thee
   Trusting thee for full salvation,
    Great and free.

Chorus.

I am trusting, trusting,
   Trusting only thee;
Saviour, Saviour,
   Trusting only thee.

2 I am trusting thee for pardon,
    At thy feet I bow;
   In thy grace and tender mercy
    Trusting now.

3 I am trusting thee for cleansing
    In the crimson flood;
   Trusting thee to make me holy
    By thy blood.

4 I am trusting thee to guide me;
    Thou alone shalt lead,
   Every day and hour supplying
    All my need.

5 I am trusting thee for power,
    These can never fail;
   Words that thou thyself shalt give me
    Must prevail.

6 I am trusting thee, Lord Jesus;
    Never let me fall;
   I am trusting thee forever,
    And for all.

Frances Ridley Havergal.

22

24 Jesus Waits to Help You.

1 Brother, leave the path of sin,
  Jesus waits to help you;
He can break the bands within,
  Jesus waits to help you.

Chorus.

Victory! victory!
Glorious, glorious victory!
Christ will break the tempter's power.
Give you victory from this hour.

2 Brother, be no more a slave,
  Jesus waits to help you;
Perfect freedom you may have,
  Jesus waits to help you.

3 Brother, come and join our band,
  Jesus waits to help you;
He will lead you by the hand,
  Jesus waits to help you.

4 Brother, will you still delay?
  Jesus waits to help you;
Take a stand for right to-day,
  Jesus waits to help you.
                          Rev. E. A. Hoffman.

25 The Morning Light.

1 O THE night of time soon shall pass away,
  And the happy, golden day will dawn,
When the pilgrim staff shall be laid
    aside,
  And the kingly crown put on.

23

Chorus.

We are watching now for the Morning
Light,
For the New Jerusalem to come;
We are waiting still for the Saviour,
Christ,
Who shall call his children home.

2 O the happy day that shall gild the hills
When the Lord shall come to earth
again!
O the happy hearts that shall welcome
him
When he comes once more to reign!

3 What a joyful time when the earth shall
gleam
In the light of an eternal day,
When the saints shall sing unto Christ,
their King,
In their golden, glad array!
A. S. Kieffer.

26
WHAT WILT THOU HAVE ME TO DO?

1 ARE you willing, my sister, my brother,
To work in the field of the Lord?
Would you gladly choose more than an-
other,
His service to gain his reward?
Seek not for a prominent station,
Your zeal or your talent to show;
But ask in some humble relation:
"Lord, what wilt thou have me to
do?"

Refrain.

What wilt thou have me to do, Lord?
What wilt thou have me to do?
I ask, seeking guidance from heaven:
Lord, what wilt thou have me to do?

2 Say not: "I am humble and lowly,
   And little can do if I would."
Remember that Jesus, the Holy, said of
   one:
   "She hath done what she could."
Some names shall, like stars, shine for-
   ever,
   Which few of this world ever knew;
They sought with most earnest endeavor:
   "Lord, what wilt thou have me to
   do?"

3 Do you pray to the "Lord of the har-
   vest,"
   That he would more laborers send
To the fields that from you are the far-
   thest,
   Neglecting those you should have
   gleaned?
Cease not in the earnest petition,
   For the laborers truly are few,
Remembering to make this addition:
   "Lord, what wilt thou have me to
   do?"   *Clayes.*

27   SWEETLY RESTING.

1 In the rifted Rock I'm resting;
   Safely sheltered, I abide;
There no foes nor storms molest me,
   While within the cleft I hide.

25

Refrain.

Now I'm resting, sweetly resting
In the cleft once made for me;
Jesus, blessèd Rock of Ages,
I will hide myself in thee.

2 Long pursued by sin and Satan,
Weary, sad, I longed for rest;
Then I found this heav'nly shelter
Opened in my Saviour's breast.

3 Peace which passeth understanding,
Joy the world can never give,
Now in Jesus I am finding;
In his smiles of love I live.

4 In the rifted Rock I'll hide me,
Till the storms of life are past;
All secure in this blest refuge,
Heeding not the fiercest blast.

Mary D. James.

28

The Land Just Across the River.

1 On earth's cold, stormy banks I stand,
And cast a wishful eye
To heaven's fair and happy land,
Where my possessions lie.

Chorus.

We will rest in the fair and happy land,
Just across on the evergreen shore,
Sing the song of Moses and the Lamb,
by and by,
And dwell with Jesus evermore.

2 O'er all these wide-extended plains
  Shines one eternal day;
There God the Son forever reigns,
  And scatters night away.

3 When shall I reach that happy place,
  And be forever blest?
When shall I see my Father's face,
  And in his bosom rest?

4 Filled with delight, my raptured soul
  Would here no longer stay;
Though death's cold waves around me
  roll,
  Fearless I'd launch away.

29   THE SAVIOUR PRECIOUS.

1 I HAVE found the Saviour precious,
  And I love him more and more;
He has rolled away my burden,
  And my mourning days are o'er;
I have found the Saviour precious,
  And I find him precious still;
And my life is consecrated
  To his service and his will.

Chorus.

I have taken up the cross,
  And will never lay it down
Till I see his face in glory,
  And receive a starry crown.

2 I have found the Saviour precious,
  And, wherever I may go,
I will bear the royal standard,
  And its colors I will show;

I am ready, if he calls me,
In the battle front to stand;
I am ready—yes, and waiting—
To fulfill my Lord's command.

3 I have found the Saviour precious;
Hallelujah! praise his name!
To a mansion in his kingdom
Through his grace the right I claim.
I have found the Saviour precious;
He has proved my dearest Friend,
And my faith can trust his promise
Of protection to the end.

James S. Apple.

30 I'M HAPPY, SO HAPPY!

1 I'M happy, so happy! no words can ex-
press
The joy and the comfort I see,
For Jesus hath purchased, through in-
finite grace,
A perfect salvation for me.

Chorus.

Saved, saved, O glory to God!
I feel the assurance divine;
Saved, saved, O glory to God!
His Spirit bears witness with mine.

2 I'm happy, so happy! while trusting in
him
Whose presence o'ershadows my way;
Who leadeth my soul by the river of
peace,
And giveth me strength as my day.

28

3 My love may be tested, my faith may be
   tried,
   The depth of its fervor to prove,
But welcome each trial, my Saviour de-
   signs,
   The gold from the dross to remove.

4 O blessed Redeemer, some day I shall
   stand
   O'erwhelmed with the light of thy
      face,
Adoring forever, and shouting thy praise,
   Because thou hast saved me by grace.
                              Lizzie Edwards.

31 Cast Thy Bread upon the Waters.

1 Cast thy bread upon the waters,
   Ye who have but scant supply;
Angel eyes will watch above it;
   You shall find it by and by!
He who in his righteous balance
   Doth each human action weigh
Will your sacrifice remember,
   Will your loving deeds repay.

2 Cast thy bread upon the waters,
   Poor and weary, worn with care,
Often sitting in the shadow,
   Have you not a crumb to spare?
Can you not to those around you
   Sing some little song of hope,
As you look with longing vision
   Through faith's mighty telescope?

3 Cast thy bread upon the waters,
   Ye who have abundant store:

29

It may float on many a billow,
　It may strand on many a shore;
You may think it lost forever,
　But, as sure as God is true,
In this life or in the other, 　.
　It will yet return to you.

4 Cast thy bread upon the waters,
　Far and wide your treasures strew;
Scatter it with willing fingers,
　Shout for joy to see it go.
For if you do closely keep it,
　It will only drag you down;
If you love it more than Jesus,
　It will keep you from your crown.

5 Cast thy bread upon the waters,
　Waft it on with praying breath,
In some distant, doubtful moment
　It may save a soul from death;
When you sleep in solemn silence,
　'Neath the morn and evening dew,
Stranger hands which you have strength-
　　ened,
　May strew lilies over you.

32　　Lost but Found.

1 O the joy that fills my heart,
O the grateful tears that start,
　When I think of Jesus' love!
How he came that he might bear
All my weight of sin and care,
　How he came from heaven above.

Chorus.

Endless praise, endless praise,
To the Lord my soul shall raise;
Lost but found, O happy strain,
Dead but now I live again.

2 Lost but found, O wondrous thought!
To his fold in mercy brought;
　Saved by grace, his grace divine,
Heir with him of bliss untold,
Soon his glory I'll behold,
　What a blessèd hope is mine.

3 Lost but found! I now can sing
Vict'ry through my Saviour King
　Vict'ry ev'ry day and hour;
Vict'ry still will be my song
When I join the ransomed throng,
　Vict'ry o'er the tempter's power.

4 O that all the world would prove
How a pardoning God can love,
　How he waits for all who come!
O that all the world might see
What his grace hath done for me!
　How he welcomes wand'rers home.
F. J. C.

33 Go Tell the World of His Love.

1 Heirs to the kingdom of Jesus the Lord,
　Go tell the world of his love;
Publish the blessings that flow from his
　word,
　Go tell the world of his love;

Love that has purchased redemption
  from sin,
Love that makes happy the spirit within
Love that will help us our conquest to
  win,
  Go tell the world of his love.

Chorus.

Go tell the world, go tell the world,
  Go tell the world of his love;
Heirs to the kingdom of Jesus the Lord,
  Go tell the world of his love.

2 Think how he labored that we might
  have rest,
  Go tell the world of his love;
Think how he suffered that we might
  be blessed,
  Go tell the world of his love:
Saved by mercy, upheld by his care,
Tell of the goodness we constantly share;
Filled with his fullness, no longer for-
  bear,
  Go tell the world of his love.

3 Plead to the lost ones to come while
  they may,
  Go tell the world of his love;
Jesus is waiting, he'll save them to-day,
  Go tell the world of his love;
Love that is nearest when earth joys are
  past,
Lighting our pathway by clouds over-
  cast;
Love that will bring us to glory at last,
  Go tell the world of his love.

Abbie Mills.

32

34 HOME AT LAST.

1 HARK the song of holy rapture,
  Hear it break from yonder strand,
Where our friends for us are waiting,
  In the golden summer land;
They have reached the port of glory,
  O'er the river they have passed,
And with millions they are shouting,
  " Home at last, home at last;"
And with millions they are shouting,
  " Home at last, home at last."

2 O the long and sweet reunion,
  Where the bells of time shall cease,
O the greeting, endless greeting,
  On the vernal heights of peace ;
Where the hoping and desponding
  Of the weary heart are past,
And we enter life eternal,
  Home at last, home at last;
And we enter life eternal,
  Home at last, home at last.

3 Look beyond, the skies are clearing;
  See, the mist dissolves away;
Soon our eyes will catch the dawning,
  Of a bright celestial day;
Soon the shadows will be lifted
  That around us now are cast,
And, rejoicing, we shall gather
  Home at last, home at last,
And, rejoicing, we shall gather
  Home at last, home at last.

Fanny J. Crosby.

35 AT THE GOLDEN LANDING.

1 FRIENDS of yore have flown to heaven,
　　Springing from the house of clay,
　Glad to gain their joyful freedom,
　　Borne by angel hands away.

Chorus.

　While on Pisgah's mount I'm standing
　　Looking toward the vernal shore,
　There I seem to see them banding,
　Just beside the golden landing,
　　Waiting to receive me o'er,
　Precious ones who went before!

2 Often at the shades of ev'ning,
　　When I sit me down to rest,
　One by one I count them over,
　　They who are in glory blessed.

3 And I seem to see their faces,
　　Beaming with celestial love,
　Shining as their blessèd Master,
　　White-robed, with the saints above.

4 And I think I hear them speaking,
　　As they often spake to me,
　While I seem to hear them saying:
　　"Pilgrim, heaven is waiting thee."

5 Brother, sister, faithful soldier,
　　If our mingling here so sweet,
　What shall be our joyous rapture
　　When we at the landing meet!

Edgar Page.

36   Work, Vote, Pray.

1 WE will work, we will work for the tem-
    perance cause,
  For the sake of the land that we love;
For the sake of the souls who are tempt-
    ed to sin,
  We will lift up our banner above.

Chorus.

We will work and pray, we will vote
    alway
For the men who will make better laws;
We will work and pray, we will labor
    night and day
For the good of the temperance cause.

2 We will pray, we will pray for the tem-
    perance cause,
  To our God ever ruling on high;
He is mightier still than the hosts of the
    foe,
  Though they gather his power to defy.

3 We will vote, we will vote for the tem-
    perance cause.
  We will rally our strength at the polls,
We'll remember the wives who are pray-
    ing at home;
  We'll remember the peril of souls.

4 As we work, as we pray, so we mean to
    vote;
  Let our watch-word ring boldly again:
Here are hearts, here are hands, here are
    courage and faith,
  And may God give his blessing, Amen.

E. E. Hewitt.

37 JOY IN HEAVEN.

1 THERE is joy among the angels,
  There's a mighty shout of rapture;
Far beyond the pearly gates the news
    has come
Of a sinner now repenting,
To the gospel-word consenting,
Of a contrite soul that seeks its better
  home.

Chorus.

Joy, joy, joy, joy in heaven,
  Souls are seeking now the living way;
There is joy, joy, joy, joy among the an-
    gels;
  Join their hallelujah songs to-day.

2 There is joy among the angels
    By the shining, crystal river,
For a wand'ring one is safe within the
    fold;
  For the Shepherd sought and found
    him,
  And the arms of love are round him ;
Hear the music gladly ring from harps
    of gold.

3 There is holy joy in heaven
    Higher, purer than the angels';
'Tis the Father's heart rejoicing in its
    love;
  'Tis the Saviour Shepherd singing
  O'er the lost one he is bringing,
Bringing to the everlasting home above.

E. E. Hewitt.

38

WE SHALL WALK THE REALMS OF GLORY.

1 WE shall walk the realms of glory,
Where eternal beauty reigns,
There with seraph hosts unnumbered
Join the grand immortal strains.

Chorus.

We shall walk the realms of glory,
With the loved ones gone before,
We shall sing the sweet old story,
Over on the other shore.

2 We shall walk the realms of glory
With the blood - washed, mighty
throng,
We shall join the angel harpers
In their everlasting song.

3 We shall walk the realms of glory,
And by Jesus' side sit down;
Clad no more in robes of sorrow,
We shall wear a fadeless gown.

4 We shall walk the realms of glory,
Where no tears can ever come,
Where the sunlight is not needed,
In that sweet, eternal home.

Emma Pitt.

39   NOT SATISFIED HERE.

1 I KNOW the joy of pardoned sin,
The witness sweet and clear;
But satisfied I have not been,
E'en with that portion fair.

Refrain.

Not satisfied here, not satisfied here,
I am not satisfied here;
Not satisfied here, not satisfied here,
I shall be satisfied there.

2 I know the cleansing from all sin,
The freedom from all care;
And yet I am not satisfied,
Nor can be, brother, here.

3 I know the blessèd shelt'ring wings,
His guiding hand so dear,
And heav'nly music through me rings,
But satisfied? Not here.

4 I run on duty's errand fleet,
I feel the Master near,
But more I long to be complete,
His perfect likeness bear!

5 No, no, my Lord, not satisfied,
'Till full redemption's given,
And the free spirit at thy side,
Shall live the life of heaven.

Rev. J. Lemacks Stokes.

40   BLESSED LIGHT OF GOD.

1 DAY by day we journey here,
In the light of God;
Shadows lift and disappear,
In the light of God,
Here his precepts we obey,
Here 'tis sweet to sing and pray,
And our hope fades not away,
In the light of God.

Chorus.

In the light,
Blessed light of God,
In the light, in the light,
Blessed light of God!
We all rejoice as we journey home,
In the light, in the light,
We all rejoice as we journey home,
In the blessèd light of God.

2 We have gospel words to speak,
In the light of God;
We have er i ig ones to seek,
In the light of God.
Life its cares and duties bring,
Yet 'tis sweet to work and sing,
As its days are on the wing,
In the light of God.

3 All our joys so sweetly blend,
In the light of God;
And our joys will never end,
In the light of God.
We have words of love and cheer,
And we never need to fear
While in faith we journey here,
In the light of God.

E. A. Barnes.

41   FATHER ALL HOLY.

The Lord's Prayer.

1 FATHER all holy, bend we so lowly,
Glowing with love's tender flame,
Father in heaven, praises be given,
Hallowed forever thy name.

Telling the story, spreading thy glory,
  Send forth thy people, we pray,
'Till ev'ry nation know thy salvation,
  Under thy kingdom's full sway.

2 Angels adore thee, waiting before thee,
  Swift thy commands to fulfill:
Grant us, we pray thee, grace to obey
    thee,
  Choosing and serving thy will.
Father, now lead us, day by day feed us,
  Ever provide and defend;
Trespass confessing, seeking thy bless-
    ing,
  Pardon and peace without end.

3 From sin deliver, keep us forever,
  Kingdom and glory are thine,
Thine too, the power, hear us this hour,
  Father, our Father divine!
Jesus is pleading, still interceding,
  For his redeemed ones again,
For his sake hear us, in his name cheei
    us,
  He is the faithful "Amen."
                              E. E. Hewitt.

42   GOD SO LOVED THE WORLD.

1 GOD loved the world so tenderly
    His only Son he gave,
  That all who on his name believe
    Its wondrous power will save
                              4C

Chorus.

For God so loved the world that he gave
  his only Son,
  That whosoever believeth in him
Should not perish, should not perish;
  That whosoever believeth in him
Should not perish, but have everlasting
  life.

2 O love that only God can feel,
    And only he can show!
  Its heighth and depth, its length and
    breadth,
  Nor heaven nor earth can know!

3 Why perish, then, ye ransomed ones?
    Why slight the gracious call?
  Why turn from him whose words pro-
    claim
  Eternal life to all?

4 O Saviour! melt these hearts of ours,
    And teach us to believe
  That whosoever comes to thee
    Shall endless life receive.
                              Fanny J. Crosby.

43   ALL IS READY.

1 "ALL is ready," the Master said,
  All is ready, the feast is spread;
  Sweet his message of love to all,
  Yet how many will slight the call!

Chorus.

Why, why, why will ye die?
Ask, and the Saviour will freely forgive;
Why, why, why will ye die?
Only a look, and your soul shall live.

2 "All is ready," he calleth still;
"Come and welcome, whoever will;"
Bring your burden of doubts and fears,
Bring your sorrow, your cares, and tears.

3 Though his mercy prolongs your day,
Time is precious, no more delay;
Now he listens to hear your prayer,
Haste the garment of praise to wear.

4 Take the pardon his love bestows,
Take the water of life that flows;
Lo! he standeth beside the door;
Hear the Spirit your hearts implore.

Sallie L. Smith.

44

LEANING ON THE EVERLASTING ARMS.

1 WHAT a fellowship, what a joy divine,
Leaning on the everlasting arms;
What a blessedness, what a peace is mine,
Leaning on the everlasting arms.

Refrain.

Leaning, leaning,
Safe and secure from all alarms;
Leaning, leaning,
Leaning on the everlasting arms

2 O how sweet to walk in this pilgrim
way,
Leaning on the everlasting arms;   .
O how bright the path grows from day
to day,
Leaning on the everlasting arms.

3 What have I to dread, what have I to
fear,
Leaning on the everlasting arms?
I have blessèd peace with my Lord so
near,
Leaning on the everlasting arms.

Rev. E. A. Hoffman.

45   TRUSTING JESUS, THAT IS ALL.

1 SIMPLY trusting ev'ry day;
Trusting though a stormy way:
Even when my faith is small,
Trusting Jesus, that is all.

Chorus.

Trusting him while life shall last,
Trusting him till earth is past,
Till within the jasper wall,
Trusting Jesus, that is all.

2 Brightly doth his Spirit shine
Into this poor heart of mine;
While he leads I cannot fall,
Trusting Jesus, that is all.

3 Singing, if my way is clear;
Praying, if the path is drear;
If in danger, for him call,
Trusting Jesus, that is all.

4 Trusting as the moments fly,
Trusting as the days go by,
Trusting him whate'er befall,
Trusting Jesus, that is all.

Edgar **Page.**

46 THE MIND OF JESUS.

1 O to have the mind of Jesus,
Purer than the light of day;
Calm as skies that smile at morning,
When the storm has passed away!

Chorus.

O to have the mind of Jesus!
O to "see him as he is!"
This our highest, holiest longing,
This is heaven's crowning bliss.

2 O to have the mind of Jesus,
With the heav'nly flame aglow,
Scatt'ring love's sweet benefactions
All around us as we go!

3 O to have the mind of Jesus,
On the Father's service bent;
Meek and lowly, true and faithful,
With the Father's will content!

4 O to have the mind of Jesus,
When, like him, the cross we bear,
Patient in " much tribulation,"
Joyful through the pow'r of prayer!

E. E. Hewitt.

47 THE CROSSINGS.

1 O THE cruel Egypt bondage
  Of my soul enslaved by sin!
  O the hopeless toil and striving,
  Foes without and foes within!

Chorus.

  O the crossings, O the crossings
  From Egypt to Canaan's shore!
  O the crossings, O the crossings!
  Saviour, lead me safely o'er.

2 Till I heard the voice of Jesus,
  Calling me to liberty:
  " I will lead you, as once Moses
  Led the people through the sea."

3 So I reached the deep sea waters,
  But by faith I soon crossed o'er;
  Lo! the wilderness of trial
  Lay this side of Canaan's shore.

4 Wand'ring, halting, fainting ever,
  Once again my Lord's command
  Called me to the Jordan crossing,
  And I reached the Promised Land.

5 Now I rest me in the bowers
  Of this holy Beulah land,
  And am kept from sin and sorrow,
  'Neath the shadow of his hand.
  Rev. J. L. Stokes.

48 I AM WEARY OF SIN.

1 I AM weary of sin, and I long to be free,
  O say, is there hope for a sinner like me?

Can I, who have strayed o'er the dark
mountain's brow,
Return to the Saviour and plead with
him now?

Chorus.

I long to be free, I long to be free;
O blessèd Redeemer, have pity on me;
The fountain lies open, and there will I
go,
And bathe in its waters till whiter than
snow.
Till whiter than snow, till whiter than
snow,
I'll bathe in its waters till whiter than
snow;
The fountain lies open, and there will I
go,
And bathe in its waters till whiter than
snow.

2 I am weary of sin, for it lures to deceive,
On thee, my Redeemer, I now will be-
lieve;
I haste as I am to the clear, flowing tide,
Where, deep in its bosom, the past thou
wilt hide.

3 I am weary of sin, and I pray to be thine,
To lean on thy word, and its promise di-
vine,
To feel in my heart thy protection and
care,
And know 'tis thy yoke and thy burden
I bear.

46

4 I am weary of sin, of its conflicts and
strife,
I sigh for a purer and happier life—
A life that is filled with the fullness of
love,
Preparing my spirit for mansions above.
Martha J. Lankton.

49   Hold On, My Soul.

1 Hold on, my soul, to the end hold out,
    With a faith no storm can shock;
Stand firm, stand fast, for the Lord has
    said
    He will hide thee in the rifted rock.

Chorus.

Hold on, hold on
    With a faith no storm can shock,
Hold on, my soul; for the Lord hath said
    He will hide thee in the rifted rock.

2 Hold on, my soul, though the lightnings
flash,
    And thy sails all torn may be;
For thy hope still points to the polar star,
    Brightly shining through the clouds
    for thee.

3 Hold on, my soul, though the waves run
high;
    For the night and storm shall cease,
There is light beyond, 'tis the morning
breaks,
    Thou art coming to the port of peace.

4 Hold on, my soul, for the end draws near,
And thy voyage is well-nigh o'er,
And the welcome home thou hast longed
to hear
Soon will greet thee on the golden
shore.

W. H. Jones.

50   Tell It to Jesus.

1 Are you weary, are you heavy-hearted?
Tell it to Jesus, tell it to Jesus;
Are you grieving over joys departed?
Tell it to Jesus alone.

Chorus.

Tell it to Jesus, tell it to Jesus,
He is a friend that's well known;
You have no other such a friend or
brother,
Tell it to Jesus alone.

2 Do the tears flow down your cheeks un-
bidden?
Tell it to Jesus, tell it to Jesus,
Have you sins that to man's eyes are
hidden?
Tell it to Jesus alone.

3 Do you fear the gath'ring clouds of sor-
row?
Tell it to Jesus, tell it to Jesus;
Are you anxious what shall be to-mor-
row?
Tell it to Jesus alone.

4 Are you troubled at the thought of dy-
　　ing?
　　Tell it to Jesus, tell it to Jesus;
　For Christ's coming kingdom are you
　　sighing?
　　Tell it to Jesus alone.
                              J. E. Rankin, D.D.

51　I'm Waiting for Thee.

1 O why dost thou linger so long
　　Outside in the danger and cold?
　Come home to the shelter and warmth;
　　Come home to the joy of the fold.

Chorus.

Come home, come home, I am calling
　　to-day;
　Come home, I am waiting for thee;
　Come home, come home, to the arms
　　of my love;
　　I am waiting, waiting for thee.

2 The light streameth out from the door,
　　Behold it, and enter and live!
　The service of love is most sweet;
　　And life everlasting I give.

3 Who comes to the fold of my care
　　Shall drink from the fountain of joy,
　And works of devotion and love
　　His heart and his hands shall employ.

4 Then come without waiting or doubt,
　　Bring all of your burdens to me;
　There's rest in the shelter of home;
　　There's rest and there's comfort for
　　thee.　　　　　*Mrs. R. N. Turner.*

4　　　　　　49

52 Redeemed, Praise the Lord.

1 O happy day! what a Saviour is mine!
  I am redeemed, praise the Lord!
All to his pleasure I gladly resign,
  I am redeemed, praise the Lord!
Jesus has taken my burden away;
Jesus has turned all my night into day,
Jesus has come to my heart—come to
    stay—
  I am redeemed, praise the Lord!

Chorus.

O happy day! what a Saviour is mine!
  I am redeemed, praise the Lord!
All to his pleasure I gladly resign,
  I am redeemed, praise the Lord!

2 O clap your hands, all ye people of God,
  I am redeemed, praise the Lord!
Let ev'ry tongue speak his mercy abroad!
  I am redeemed, praise the Lord!
His loving-kindness is better than gold!
He doth bestow more than my cup can
    hold!
Wondrous salvation, that ne'er can be
    told—
  I am redeemed, praise the Lord!

3 Thanks be to God for the great vict'ry
    given,
  I am redeemed, praise the Lord!
Now I am free; ev'ry chain has been
    riven—
  I am redeemed, praise the Lord!

Out of the pit and the mire and the clay,
Jesus has born me in triumph away;
Safe on the Rock I am standing to-day—
 I am redeemed, praise the Lord!

4 "Glory to God!" I would shout evermore,
 I am redeemed, praise the Lord!
O for a voice that could reach ev'ry shore,
 I am redeemed, praise the Lord!
Help me, ye ransomed, awake ev'ry
  string,
Let earth rejoice, and the whole heavens
  ring,
While we the chorus unitedly sing:
 "I am redeemed, praise the Lord!"
                                    Abbie Mills.

53 Come to Jesus While You May.

1 Come to Jesus, trembling sinner,
 With your load of guilt oppressed;
Come to Jesus, he will save you;
 Come, and he will give you rest.

Chorus.

Come to Jesus, come to Jesus,
 Weary sinner, come to Jesus while
  you may;
He will save you, he will save you,
 Weary sinner, he will save you; come
  to-day.

2 He is waiting, he is ready,
 Tender, loving words to say;
Will you not accept his blessing?
 Give your heart to him to-day?

3 Time is flying, do not tarry,
Haste while it is called to-day!
Can you spurn his tender pleading?
Can you turn this friend away?

4 Do not linger, do not trifle,
Heed your loving Saviour's call;
In his tender heart there's mercy,
In his arms there's room for all.

Mrs. C. N. Pickop.

54 THE SAVIOUR IS MY ALL IN ALL.

1 THE Saviour is my all in all,
He is my constant theme!
By simply trusting in his word
He keeps me pure and clean.

Chorus.

Glory! O glory!
Jesus hath redeemed me;
Glory! O glory!
He washed my sins away.

2 His Spirit gives sweet peace within,
And bids all care depart!
He fills my soul with righteousness,
And purifies the heart.

3 And whatsoever I may ask,
To glorify his name,
The Father freely gives to me,
Since Christ the Saviour came.

4 O praise the Lord, my soul, rejoice,
Give thanks unto thy God!
Who took thee in thy sinfulness,
And cleansed thee by his blood!

P. Bilhorn.

55   Free Waters.

1 There's a fountain free, 'tis for you and
me:
Let us haste, O haste to its brink;
'Tis the fount of love from the source
above,
And he bids us all freely drink.

Chorus.

Will you come to the fountain free?
Will you come? 'tis for you and me;
Thirsty soul, hear the welcome call:
'Tis a fountain opened for all.

2 There's a living stream, with a crystal
gleam:
From the throne of life now it flows;
While the waters roll let the weary soul
Hear the call that forth freely goes.

3 There's a living well, and its waters swell,
And eternal life they can give;
And we joyful sing, ever spring, O spring,
As we haste to drink and to live.

4 There's a rock that's cleft, and no soul is
left
That may not its pure waters share;
'Tis for you and me, and its stream I see:
Let us hasten joyfully there.
Mrs. M. B. C. Slade.

56. Jesus Is Calling for Thee.

1 O come, to Calvary turning,
Jesus is calling for thee;
His heart so tenderly yearning,
Jesus is calling for thee.

Come now, and enter the fountain,
Fountain of mercy so free;
Though sin arise like a mountain,
Jesus is calling for thee.

Chorus.

Calling, calling,
Jesus is calling for thee;
Calling, calling,
Jesus is calling for thee.

2 O hark! in life's sunny morning,
Jesus is calling for thee;
Sweet flowers thy pathway adorning,
Jesus is calling for thee.
He sends thee gladness and pleasure,
Wilt thou not thank him to-day?
Come now, and seek endless treasure,
Joys that are brighter than day.

3 O soul so burdened and weary,
Jesus is calling for thee;
He'll lift the shadows so dreary,
Jesus is calling for thee.
In love thy troubles are given:
Sorrow is only his voice,
That bids thee look up to heaven;
Look, and in Jesus rejoice!

4 But still the Saviour is calling,
Jesus is calling for thee;
Though now the night-dews are fall·
ing,
Jesus is calling for thee.

E'en though so long thou hast slight-
 ed—
Slighted salvation so great,
Yet his own promise is plighted,
Come; Jesus stands at the gate.
Lidie H. Edmunds.

57   PURITY, WHITER THAN SNOW.

1 INTO the fountain of cleansing we go,
Down where the waters of purity flow,
Troubled to-day is that fountain, we
 know,
Washing us whiter than snow.

Refrain.

Whiter than snow, whiter than snow,
Come where the waters of purity flow,
Wash and be whiter than snow.

2 O what a wonderful power is there,
Saving the soul from its utter despair,
Washing and cleansing we all now may
 share,
Purity, whiter than snow!

3 Here by this Fount of Salvation we stay,
Open for sin and uncleanness to-day,
Guilt and corruption are banished away,
Purity, whiter than snow.

4 Christ has revealed his deep love to my
 soul,
Now by his merits my heart is made
 whole.
Wide are the waves of his fullness that
 roll;
Purity, whiter than snow.
Rev. John O. Foster.

58 There's a Beautiful Land.

1 There's a beautiful land on high,
To its glories I fain would fly—
When by sorrows pressed down,
I long for my crown
In that beautiful land on high.

Refrain.
In that beautiful land I'll be,
From earth and its cares set free;
My Jesus is there, he's gone to pre-
A place in that land for me.   [pare

2 There's a beautiful land on high,
I shall enter it by and by,
There, with friends hand in hand,
I shall walk on the strand
In that beautiful land on high.

3 There's a beautiful land on high,
Then why should I fear to die,
When death is the way to the realms
of day?
In that beautiful land on high.

4 There's a beautiful land on high,
And my kindred its bliss enjoy;
Methinks I now see how they're wait-
ing for me
In that beautiful land on high.

5 There's a beautiful land on high;
And, though here I oft weep and sigh,
My Jesus hath said that no tears shall
be shed
In that beautiful land on high.

6 There's a beautiful land on high,
  Where we never shall say good-by!
    When over the river we are happy
    forever,
  In that beautiful land on high.
James Nicholson.

59 Gather the Reapers Home,

1 Have ye heard the song from the gold-
    en land?
  Have ye heard the glad new song?
  Let us bind our sheaves with a willing
    hand,
  For the time will not be long.

                Refrain.
  The Lord of the harvest will soon ap-
    pear,
  His smile, his voice we shall see and
    hear;
  The Lord of the harvest will soon ap-
    pear
  And gather the reapers home.

2 They are looking down from the golden
    land,
  Our belovèd are looking down;
  They have done their work, they have
    born their cross,
  And received their promised crown.

3 O the song rolls on from the golden land,
  And our hearts are strong to-day,
  For it nerves our souls with its music
    sweet,
  And we toil in the noontide ray.

4 O the song rolls on from the golden land
  From its vales of joy and flowers,
  And we feel and know by a living faith,
  That its tones will soon be ours.

Jennie Johnson.

60   Meet Me There.

1 On the happy, golden shore,
  Where the faithful part no more,
  When the storms of life are o'er,
    Meet me there;
  Where the night dissolves away
  Into pure and perfect day,
  I am going home to stay.
    Meet me there.

Chorus.

Meet me there,
Meet me there,
Where the tree of life is blooming,
  Meet me there;
When the storms of life are o'er,
On the happy golden shore,
Where the faithful part no more,
  Meet me there.

2 Here our fondest hopes are vain,
  Dearest links are rent in twain;
  But in heav'n no throb of pain,
    Meet me there;
  By the river, sparkling bright,
  In the city of delight,
  Where our faith is lost in sight,
    Meet me there.

3 Where the harps of angels ring,
And the blest forever sing,
In the palace of the King,
  Meet me there;
Where, in sweet communion, blend
Heart with heart, and friend with
  friend,
In a world that ne'er shall end,
  Meet me there.
                              Henrietta E. Blair.

61   Go Save a Poor Sinner.

1 I'll sing of the story, how Jesus from
  glory
Has saved a poor sinner like me;
That all who believe him, and all who
  receive him,
His blessèd salvation may see.

Chorus.

Then sing the glad chorus,
His banner is o'er us,
  His mercy is boundless and free;
From heaven descended,
His love is extended,
  To save a poor sinner like me. .

2 His glory immortal, bright over the por-
  tal,
Has banished the gloom from the
  grave;
The Lord has ascended, the darkness is
  ended,
And now he is mighty to save.

59

3 Though seasons of error, and moments
   of terror,
   Like billows of sorrow may roll;
   In Christ I'm confiding, in him I am
   hiding,
   With safety and rest to my soul.

4 My peace like a river flows onward for-
   ever,
   A tide to eternity's sea;
   To swell the old story with voices in
   glory,
   He saved a poor sinner like me.
                          Rev. John O. Foster, A.M.

62   The Lights of Home.

1 Steersman, steersman, the channel's
   rough and dark,
   The waves roll high, the winds sweep
   by,
   Now whither speeds thy bark?
   Now whither speeds thy bark?
      Sailing, sailing, to reach a glorious
      home,
   Though storms assail, we dare the gale,
   For Jesus bids us come.

Chorus.

Sailing o'er the restless tide,
Sailing through the gale we glide,
There beyond the billows' foam
We see the lights of home.

2 Steersman, steersman, the stars **are**
　　wrapped in mist,
The Polar star still beams afar
On hills of amethyst,
On hills of amethyst.　　　　.
　Sailing, sailing, to find a better land,
No wind that blows our hope o'erthrows,
　While Christ waits on the strand.

3 Steersman, steersman, how wild the tem-
　　pest raves!
The floods may swell, but all is well,
While Jesus walks the waves,
While Jesus walks the waves.
　Sailing, sailing, to find a happier
　　shore,
A pathway bright shines through the
　　night,
　Where friends have gone before.
　　　　　　　Priscilla J. Owens.

63　　Battling for the Lord.

Semi-chorus.

1 We've listed in a holy war,
　Battling for the Lord!
Eternal life our guiding star,
　Battling for the Lord!

Full Chorus.

We'll work till Jesus comes,
We'll work till Jesus comes,
We'll work till Jesus comes,
And then we'll rest at home.

61

2 We've girded on our armor bright,
  Battling for the Lord!
  Our Captain's word our strength and
    might,
  Battling for the Lord!

3 We'll stand like heroes on the field,
  Battling for the Lord!
  And nobly fight, but never yield,
  Battling for the Lord!

4 Though sin and death our way oppose,
  Battling for the Lord!
  Through grace we'll conquer all our foes,
  Battling for the Lord!

5 And when our glorious war is o'er,
  Battling for the Lord!
  We'll shout salvation evermore,
  Battling for the Lord!

64   In the Book of Life.

1 In thy book, where glory bright
  Shines with never-fading light,
  Where thy saved thou wilt record,
  Write my name, my name, O Lord.

Chorus.

Write my name in the book of Life,
  Lamb of God, write it there;
Where thy saved thou wilt record,
Write my name, my name, O Lord.

2 In the book, whose pages tell
  Who have tried to serve thee well,
  O'er my name let mercy trace:
  "Child of God, redeemed by grace."

3 In the book, where thou dost keep
Record still of years that sleep,
Let my name be written down,
Heir to life's immortal crown.

4 O my Saviour, thou canst show
What I long so much to know:
Let my faith behold and see
That my life is hid with thee.
Lizzie Edwards.

65   Mansions All Bright.

1 O when shall I dwell in a mansion all
bright,
And Jesus, my Saviour, behold?
Or walk by his side, like an angel of
light,
In a city all garnished with gold.

Chorus.

Home of the blest!
Home of the blest!
When wilt thou ever be mine?
Home of the blest!
Home of the blest!
Soon shalt thou ever be mine.

2 No pearl from the ocean or gold from
the mine
Can pardon or purity buy:
I'll trust in the blood of a Saviour di-
vine,
And cling to the cross till I die.

63

3 But while I am a stranger away from
      my home,
   I'll toil in the vineyard and pray;
   I'll carry the cross while I think of the
      crown,
   And watch for the break of the day.

66   I COME TO THEE.

1 FROM yonder cross what beams divine
   Of peace and hope and mercy shine!
   O be each blessèd promise mine!
   I come, dear Lord, to thee.

Chorus.

    I come to thee,
    I come to thee;
   Thine outstretched arms I see;
    I come to thee,
   Dear Lord, who died for me.

2 Thy kind, inviting voice I know;
   Thy wounded hands new life bestow:
   Those hands will never let me go;
   I come, dear Lord, to thee.

3 As seeks the weary bird its nest
   When the sunset lingers in the west,
   So now for pardon, healing, rest,
   I come, dear Lord, to thee.

4 'Midst pressing care and daily need
   Thy overruling love I read,
   For help, thy "present help," I plead;
   I come, dear Lord, to thee.

5 In weakness be my mighty Tower,
  My Refuge in temptation's hour;
  My brightest joy when blessings shower;
  I come, dear Lord, to thee.

E. E. Hewitt.

67   Speak to Me, Jesus.

1 Speak to me, Jesus, I'm far from thy fold;
  Far from kind friends that so often have
    told
  That story so simple, so kind, and so
    free,
  O speak to me, Jesus, I'll listen to thee.

Chorus.

Speak to me, Jesus, speak from above,
Tell of thy hands, of thy side, and thy
  love;
Forget not thy blood that from sin makes
  so free;
O speak to me, Jesus, I will come to thee.

2 Speak to me, Jesus, in tones that so oft,
  In sickness and sorrow, so tender and
    soft,
  Did gently admonish in Bethany's home,
  O speak to me, Jesus, to thee I will come.

3 Speak to me, Jesus, O tell of thy power,
  Mighty to save when my wand'rings are
    o'er;
  I seek now for pardon, in penitence
    wait;
  O speak to me, Jesus, before 'tis too late.

Chorus.

Speak to me, Jesus, speak from above,
Tell of thy hands, of thy side, and thy
love;
Forget not thy blood that from sin makes
so free;
O speak to me, Jesus, I now come to
thee.

4 Speak to me, Jesus, thy Spirit impart,
To strengthen, to comfort and cheer my
weak heart;
Thy voice I have heard, and thy blood
is applied,
O help me, dear Saviour, to live at thy
side.

Chorus.

Speak to me, Jesus, speak from above,
Tell of thy hands, of thy side, and thy
love;
Forget not thy blood that from sin makes
so free;
O speak to me, Jesus, I have come to
thee.   *H. L. Gilmour.*

68   COME OVER.

1 COME over, lost one, come
Over the line to-day,
Where Jesus bids you stand;
O come away.

Chorus.

Come over, O come over,
Come over the line to-day;
And heav'n delight, while men invite,
And angels seem to say:

Come over, O come over,
  Come over the line to-day;
To Jesus bow, he calls you now,
  Come over the line to-day.

2 Only a step to God,
  One step to cross the line;
Hasten, O dying one.
  Touch the Divine!

3 Moment of priceless worth,
  When God has drawn so near;
His wondrous tenderness,
  Sinner, revere.

4 Dare not this call refuse,
  When duty is so plain;
The Spirit long denied
  Comes not again.

5 Lost one, this call to you
  May be the very last!
Haste! e'er forevermore
  Your day be past.
                    F. A. Blackmer.

69   ENTIRE CONSECRATION.

1 TAKE my life, and let it be
Consecrated, Lord, to thee;
Take my hands, and let them move
At the impulse of thy love.

Chorus.

Wash me in the Saviour's precious blood,
Cleanse me in its purifying flood,
Lord, I give to thee my life and all, to be
Thine henceforth, eternally.

2 Take my feet, and let them be
Swift and beautiful for thee;
Take my voice, and let me sing
Always, only for my King.

3 Take my lips, and let them be
Filled with messages for thee;
Take my silver and my gold—
Not a mite would I withhold.

4 Take my moments and my days,
Let them flow in endless praise;
Take my intellect, and use
Ev'ry power as thou shalt choose.

5 Take my will, and make it thine;
It shall be no longer mine;
Take my heart—it is thine own—
It shall be thy royal throne.

6 Take my love, my Lord, I pour
At thy feet its treasure-store!
Take myself, and I will be
Ever, only, all for thee!
Frances Ridley Havergal.
Chorus by *W. J. Kirkpatrick.*

70   Walking and Talking.

1 I am saved through the blood of my crucified Lord,
With his children my lot I have cast;
I will lift up my voice, I will sing and
rejoice
That from death unto life I have
passed.
68

Refrain.

I am walking, I am talking with my
 Lord and King
In the shadow of the cross all the day,
I am walking, I am talking with my
 Lord and King,
He is leading me by faith all the way.

2 I am saved through the blood of my cru-
 cified Lord,
And the glory to him will I give;
For the grace he bestows, and his good-
 ness that flows,
I will praise him as long as I live.

3 Though the tempter assail, yet he can-
 not prevail,
I am under my Saviour's control;
And the more I believe, still the more I
 receive
Of his fullness of joy in my soul.

4 Through his wonderful love, my Re-
 deemer above,
Is preparing a mansion for me,
Where from toil I shall rest with the
 happy and blest,
And forever his face I shall see.
Sallie Smith.

71   Sweet Day of the Lord.

1 Sweet day of the Lord, we hail thee
 with joy,
We welcome thee gladly once more;
Above all the cares and labors of life,
Our songs of devotion shall soar.

Refrain.

Up to the presence of Infinite Love,
  We rise in our worship to-day;
Asking his blessing, his blessing divine,
  We joyfully bear it away.

2 O bright is the hour, when spent in his
    house,
    And precious the moments of peace;
  The flame of our hearts shall kindle
    anew,
    And love and devotion increase.

3 The Lord in his house abideth to-day,
    His Spirit gives comfort to all;
  Then come, ask for mercy, pardon, and
    grace,
    Give heed to his sweet, loving call.

4 Sweet day of the Lord, sweet Sabbath
    on earth,
    Thy hours of refreshment we love;
  Our songs shall ascend in rapture and
    praise,
    And soar in their fullness above.

Mrs. R. N. Turner.

72   Glorious as the Light.

1 When the jewels of earth shall be gath-
    ered,
    They with glory effulgent shall shine,
  As they come to the gates of that city,
    Sweeping in through its portals divine.

Chorus.

Glorious as the light of the kingdom,
Glorious as the bright, rising sun;
O what a rapt'rous sight, in that heav'nly
home so bright—
As glorious as the light of the kingdom.

2 What a host there will be of the saved
ones!
Like the stars of the night, we are told,
As they march in their strength and
their grandeur,
Through the bright, shining streets of
pure gold.

3 They are those who have followed the
Saviour,
Out of every nation and tribe,
Who have come through a great tribu-
lation,
Praises loud they to Jesus ascribe.

4 "Thou art worthy, O Christ," they are
singing,
"Who hath died, all our race to re-
deem."
"Hallelujah!" the grand swelling cho-
rus,
And his love everlasting their theme.
L. W. Smith.

73   Stepping-stones to Jesus.

1 Stepping-stones to Jesus
All our joys may be,
Used with glad thanksgiving
For his love so free.

71

Many, many blessings
    In our paths may fall,
Stepping-stones to Jesus,
    We may find them all.

Chorus.

Looking for the stepping-stones
    Placed along life's way;
Looking for the stepping-stones,
    We find them every day;
Stepping-stones to Jesus,
Stepping-stones to Jesus,
Looking for the stepping-stones,
    We find them every day.

2 Stepping-stones to Jesus,
    Leading to his feet,
Are the little trials,
    Which we daily meet;
Ev'ry need that presses,
    Ev'ry vexing care,
Ev'ry disappointment,
    Ev'ry cross we bear.

3 Stepping-stones to Jesus,
    All the pure delight,
In his works of beauty,
    All things fair and bright.
Ev'ry sweet affection,
    Tender human love
Brought in consecration
    To the Friend above.

4 Stepping-stones to Jesus,
    Bless&d means of grace;
Prayer and sweet communion
    In the sacred place;

Ev'ry self-denial
  For the Master's cause,
Each renewed obeying
  Of his holy laws.

E. E. Hewitt.

74   Gathered Home.

1 Shall we all meet at home in the morn-
    ing,
  On the shore of the bright crystal sea,
With the loved ones who long have been
    waiting?
  What a meeting indeed that will be!

Refrain.

  Gathered home,
  Gathered home,
On the shores of the bright, crystal sea;
  Gathered home,
  Gathered home,
With the loved ones forever to be.

2 Shall we all meet at home in the morn-
    ing,
  And from sorrow forever be free?
Shall we join in the songs of the ran-
    somed?
  What a meeting indeed that will be!

3 Shall we all meet at home in the morn-
    ing,
  There our blessèd Redeemer to see?
Shall we know and be known by our
    loved ones?
  What a meeting, indeed, that will be!

Selected.

75 KEEP ME EVER CLOSE TO THEE.

SOURCE from whence the streams of
    mercy
    Like a river flow to me,
With thy cords of love so tender
    Bind and keep me close to thee.

Refrain.

Keep me ever close to thee,
Blessèd Saviour, dear to me,
With thy cords of love so tender
Bind and keep me close to thee;
Keep me ever close to thee,
Blessèd Saviour, dear to me,
Bind and keep me close to thee.

2 There my life, my hope and comfort,
    There a refuge for my soul
When the clouds hang darkly round me,
    And the distant surges roll.

3 There, in holy, sweet communion
    With thy Spirit day by day,
Faith to realms of light and glory
    Bears my raptured soul away.

4 Close to thee, O Saviour, keep me,
    Till I reach the shining shore,
Till I join the raptured army,
    Shouting joy forever more.
Fanny J. Crosby.

76 and 77 SING ON.

1 SING on, ye joyful pilgrims,
    Nor think the moments long;
My faith is heav'nward rising
    With ev'ry tuneful song;

Lo! on the mount of blessing,
  The glorious mount, I stand,
And looking o'er the river,
  I see the heav'nly land.

Chorus.

Sing on, O blissful music!
  With ev'ry note you raise
My heart is filled with rapture,
  My soul is lost in praise.
Sing on, O blissful music!
  With ev'ry note you raise
My heart is filled with rapture,
  My soul is lost in praise.

2 Sing on, ye joyful pilgrims,
    While here on earth we stay
  Let songs of home and Jesus
    Beguile each fleeting day;
  Sing on the grand old story
    Of his redeeming love,
  The everlasting chorus
    That fills the realms above.

3 Sing on, ye joyful pilgrims:
    The time will not be long
  Till in our Father's kingdom
    We swell a nobler song,
  Where those we love are waiting
    To greet us on the shore,
  We'll meet beyond the river,
    Where surges roll no more.
                    Carrie M. Wilson.

78   Up and Onward.

1 Up for Jesus! up and onward!
    Hear him saying "follow me;"
  In the noble Christian army
    Faithful soldiers let us be.

Chorus.

  Marching on with singing,
  Sweetest music bringing
      Unto him that shall reign;
  Let the world before us
  Hear the joyful chorus,
      Hallelujah, Amen.

  Up for Jesus! up and onward!
    In the early morning bright,
  With the watch-word on our banner,
    Brave defenders of the right.

3 Up for Jesus! up and onward!
    Through the conflict firmly stand;
  For we cannot lose a battle
    With our leader in command.

4 Up for Jesus! up and onward!
    He will guide us with his eye;
  He has promised if we trust him,
    We shall conquer by and by.
                      Sallie Martin.

79 No Shade Like This for Me.

1 Oppressed with noonday's searching
      heat,
    To yonder cross I flee;
  Beneath its shelter take my seat,
    No shade like this for me.

Refrain.

No shade like this for me,
No shade like this for me;
Beneath its shelter take my seat,
No shade like this for me.

2 Beneath that cross clear waters burst,
   A fountain sparkling free;
And there I quench my desert thirst,
   No spring like this for me.

Refrain.

No spring like this for me,
No spring like this for me;
And there I quench my desert thirst,
No spring like this for me.

3 A stranger here I pitch my tent,
   Beneath this spreading tree;
Here shall my pilgrim life be spent,
   No home like this for me.

Refrain.

No home like this for me,
No home like this for me;
Here shall my pilgrim life be spent,
No home like this for me.

4 For burdened ones a resting-place
   Beside that cross I see;
I here cast off my weariness,
   No rest like this for me.

77

Refrain.

No rest like this for me,
No rest like this for me;
I here cast off my weariness,
No rest like this for me.

Rev. Horatius Bonar.

80   Thine Forever.

1 Thine forever, thine forever,
   My Redeemer, will I be;
On the altar lies my off'ring,
   Consecrated now to thee;
All my fervent soul's devotion
   To thy service, Lord, I give;
For thy honor and thy glory
   I will labor while I live.

Chorus.

Thine forever, thine forever,
   Saviour, I am resting in thy love;
Thine forever, thine forever,
   Saviour, I am resting sweetly in thy
   love.

2 Thine forever, thine forever—
   O the rapture of my heart!
Thou my refuge and my comfort,
   Thou my lasting portion art;
Casting ev'ry weight behind me,
   I the Christian race will run,
Trusting thee and taking courage,
   Till the race my soul has won.

3 Where thou leadest I will follow,
  Where thou bid'st me I will go;
In the very front of battle
  Fearless will I meet the foe;
I shall conquer through thy mercy,
  I shall triumph through thy might,
I shall see thee in thy kingdom;
  There will faith be lost in sight.
Fanny J. Crosby.

81   Will You Come?

1 Hear the earnest invitation,
  Wand'rer from the path of right,
Jesus offers his salvation;
  Will you come to Christ to-night?

Chorus.

Will you come? will you come?
  Come and at his altar bow;
Will you come? will you come?
  Jesus waits to save you now.

2 Christian souls are fervent praying,
  Holy Spirit, send thy light,
Why afar in darkness straying?
  Why not come to Christ to-night?

3 Angels near us, eager bending,
  Friends beloved from homes of light,
With our hearts their question blend-
    ing,
  Will you come to Christ to-night?

4 Hear the Saviour interceding,
  Nor his gracious message slight;
Will you pass his cross unheeding?
  O return to Christ to-night.
Priscilla J. Owens.

79

82 I Will Trust in My Saviour.

1 Though the shadows gather o'er my
  pathway here,
And no sun comes with joyous ray,
In the darkness not an evil will I fear,
For my Saviour is leading the way.

Refrain.

I will trust in my Saviour,
I will trust in my Saviour,
  I will trust in my Saviour alway;
He will lead me through the night,
By his ever-shining light,
  I will trust in my Saviour to-day.

2 In the tempest when the winds around
  me roll,
And the thunders my heart affright,
Sweetly comes a loving whisper to my
  soul,
Then the world is all beauty and light.

3 When the chilling blight of death is on
  my brow,
And the earth passes from my view,
Simply trusting in my Saviour then, as
  now,
He will lead me in paths ever new.

Mrs. Loula K. Rogers.

83

Come and Ask Jesus to Save You.

1 Would you find the way to heaven?
  Come and ask Jesus to save you;
Would you know your sins forgiven?
  Come and ask Jesus to save you.

He will light and joy impart
To your dark and weary heart,
He will bid your sin depart,
Come and ask Jesus to save you.

Chorus.

Come to the fountain of mercy to-day,
Come and your sins shall be taken away;
Come to the Saviour and earnestly pray,
Jesus will certainly save you.

2 Would you treasures have above?
Come and ask Jesus to save you;
Would you know the wealth of love?
Come and ask Jesus to save you.
Come, your loving father meet;
See, he waits his child to greet;
Hasten on with eager feet;
Come and ask Jesus to save you.

3 Would you from your chains be free?
Come and ask Jesus to save you;
Would you cease a slave to be?
Come and ask Jesus to save you.
He is ev'ry captive's friend;
If on him you now depend,
His right arm will you defend,
Come and ask Jesus to save you.

4 Would you gain yon heav'nly shore?
Come and ask Jesus to save you;
Would you join those gone before?
Come and ask Jesus to save you.
He that lives who once was dead
Bore the cross; for you he bled;
He can soothe your dying bed,
Come and ask Jesus to save you.

Abbie Mills.

6   81

84   THE GLORY LAND.

1 THERE'S a land of love shining far above,
   In the endless glory of day,
And I long to know all the good who go
   To that radiant land far away.

Refrain.

O the glories there are so bright and
   fair,
Here no longer would I roam;
How my spirit sighs for the cloudless
   skies,
Of that happy, heavenly home!

2 O I love to sing of the hearts that cling
   To the light of that golden shore,
Starry crowns they'll wear and its glo-
   ries share
With the happy ones gone before.

3 And I love to dream of the crystal gleam
   Resting on the bright river there,
Of the white-robed throng and the glad
   new song,
And the fadeless flowers so fair.

4 There shall be no night! O the blessèd
   light
That illumes the heavenly shore!
No more sorrow there, and no cross to
   bear;
All is joy and peace evermore.

Mrs. Loula K. Rogers.

85   Glory, I'm Redeemed.

1 On the Saviour I've believed,
Gracious pardon I've received,
   And his blood now covers all my
     guilt and shame;
In my soul to dwell he designs,
Without rival there he reigns,
   Glory hallelujah to his name!

Chorus.

   I'm redeemed, I'm redeemed,
     In his power the Saviour came,
   And from sin gave sweet release,
   Filled my soul with heavenly peace,
     Glory, glory, hallelujah to his name!

2 When I heard his loving voice,
How it made my heart rejoice!
   Like sweet music to my longing soul it
     came;
O how wondrous, full, and free
Was his pard'ning love to me!
   Glory, glory, hallelujah to his name!

3 All along my pilgrim way
I will trust him and obey,
   And each day I'll seek to spread my
     Saviour's fame;
To exalt, my aim shall be,
Him who did so much for me,
   Glory, glory, hallelujah to his name!

4 Wondrous comfort does he send,
Proving such a constant friend,
   For he comes to bless in ev'ry need
     the same;

Empty turns me not away,
But new blessings sends each day,
  Glory, glory, hallelujah to his name!

F. A. Blackmer.

86 Fire Away with Your Ballots.

1 You need not wait any longer
    For the temp'rance bugle to blow,
  The call is louder and stronger,
    You'll hear the trumpet I know.
  The long, deep roll has been sounded,
    A signal boom from the gun;
  The staff and banner surrounded,
    And vict'ry sure to be won.

Chorus.

Fire away, fire away with your ballots,
  Fire away, fire away on the field;
Fire away, fire away, fire away, fire away,
  Fire away, fire away, till they yield.

2 The judges made their decision,
    For the laws are wholesome and
      strong;
  No longer any division,
    For liquor selling is wrong.
  The work is squarely before us,
    The great decree handed down;
  We'll fire a thundering chorus
    In ev'ry city and town.

3 March on and go for a levy,
    Break up the horrible crime;
  Give law and gospel heavy,
    A double barrel at a time.

Take aim awhile, be steady,
Be sure your aiming is low;
And shoot whenever you're ready,
And then the saloon will go.
Rev. John O. Foster, A.M.

87 GENTLE SHEPHERD, SAVE ME NOW.

1 FAR away my steps have wandered,
On the rugged mountain's brow;
But to thee my heart is crying,
Gentle Shepherd, save me now!

Chorus.

Save me now, save me now!
Gentle Shepherd, save me now!
Unto thee my heart is crying,
Gentle Shepherd, save me now!

2 Thou hast borne my weight of sorrow,
At thy feet I humbly bow;
And my heart with thee is pleading,
Gentle Shepherd, save me now!

3 Though thy love I long have slighted,
Though ungrateful I have been,
To thy fold my faith has brought me;
Let my weary soul come in.

4 Though thy love I long have slighted,
O'er my wasted years I weep;
In thy blessèd arms of mercy
Shield and save thy wand'ring sheep.
Henrietta E. Blair.

88 Songs in the Calm, Still Night.

1 'Tis the Lord who leadeth me still,
'Tis he who controls and governs my
will,
Crowns my life with holy delight,
And giveth me songs in the calm, still·
night.

Chorus.

O my soul, how favored thou art,
Thus to come so near his heart;
There by faith I walk in his light,
Who giveth me songs in the calm,
still night.

2 'Tis the Lord who whispers to me,
"I offered myself a ransom for thee;
Say, what mean thy doubtings and fears?
I carry thy sorrows and count thy tears."

3 Safe in him, I will not repine,
Though trials and cares may sometimes
be mine;
He I know will guide me aright
Who giveth me songs in the calm, still
night.

4 Safe in him, my hope and my all,
Who tenderly hears whenever I call,
Safe in him, my burden is light,
He giveth me song in the calm, still night.

Jennie Garnett.

89 In the Hush of Early Morning.

1 In the hush of early morning,
When the breeze is whisp'ring low,
There's a voice that gently calls me,
And its accents well I know!

86

Here I am, O Saviour, waiting,
  For thy will alone is mine,
This is all my crown and glory,
  I am thine and only thine!

2 When the noontide falls upon me,
    With its fervid lightning ray,
  There's a voice divinely earnest,
    Bids me work while it is day;
  Open, Saviour, now before me
    All thy will for me to do,
  Only help me, watching, working,
    Still to keep my Lord in view!

3 As the dewy shades steal downward,
    O'er the earth at ev'ning mild,
  There's a voice I love that whispers:
    "After labor rest, my child!"
  O my Saviour, loving, tender,
    Help me to account it blest
  Thus to work within thy vineyard,
    Till thou callest me to rest.
                    Mrs. R. N. Turner.

90   SHIP OF ZION.

1 THERE's a wail from the islands of the sea,
  There's a voice that is calling you and
      me,
  In the old ship of Zion,
  The strong help of Zion,
  The good news of Zion, carry ye!
  "Come over and help us!" is the cry;
  "Come over and help us! or we die,"
  I see the woe falling, I hear the voice
      calling,
  O ship of salvation, thither fly.

87

2 There's a moan from the desert, full of
   pain,
There's a sigh over Afric's sunny plain,
In the old ship of Zion,
The strong help of Zion,
Bear good news of Zion o'er the main.
"Come over and help us!" is the cry;
"Come over and help us, or we die!"
Across the wide waters
Hear Afric's dark daughters!
O ship of salvation, thither fly.

3 There's a groan from the Ganges where
   they fall,
At the feet of the idols in their thrall;
In the old ship of Zion,
The strong help of Zion,
The good news of Zion bear them all.
"Come over and help us!" is the cry;
"Come over and help us, or we die!"
I see idols falling,
And India calling,
O ship of salvation, thither fly.
                          Mrs. M. B. C. Slade.

91   CLING TO THE MIGHTY ONE.

1 CLING to the Mighty One,
     Cling in thy grief;
   Cling to the Holy One,
     He gives relief:
   Cling to the Gracious One,
     Cling in thy pain;
   Cling to the Faithful One,
     He will sustain.

2 Cling to the Living One,
    Cling in thy woe;
Cling to the Loving One,
    Through all below:
Cling to the Pard'ning One,
    He speaketh peace;
Cling to the Healing One,
    Anguish shall cease.

3 Cling to the Bleeding One,
    Cling to his side;
Cling to the Risen One,
    In Him abide;
Cling to the coming One,
    Hope shall arise;
Cling to the Reigning One,
    Joy lights thine eyes.

92   The Clear Light of Heaven.

1 In darkness I wandered till Jesus I
  found,
And then, praise his name! and then,
  praise his name!
The clear light of heaven my pathway
  shone round,
And peace to my spirit there came.

Chorus.

And now I'm confiding,
And sweetly abiding
In Jesus, my Saviour,
Companion, and Guide:
His name I'm confessing.
He fills me with blessing;
To me he's far dearer
Than all else beside.

89

2 The birds over my head seemed to
   sing a new song,
      So wondrously sweet, so wondrously
      sweet;
   All nature seemed praising in notes loud
      and long,
      My Saviour, when first we did meet.

3 And now we are walking together
   along,
      My Saviour and I, my Saviour and I;
   He blesses and leads me with hand
      kind and strong,
      And freely his grace does supply.

4 O wonderful Brother, Redeemer, and
   Friend!
      I love him I know, I love him I
      know,
   This blessèd companionship, never to
      end,
      Grows sweeter as onward I go.
                              F. A. Blackmer.

93   Sing Hallelujah.

1 When Jesus washed my sins away,
      Sing hallelujah!
   My happy heart began to say,
      Praise ye the Lord.

Chorus.

Sing hallelujah! sing hallelujah!
Sing hallelujah! praise ye the Lord.

2 He makes my wounded spirit whole,
      Sing hallelujah!
   He satisfies my longing soul,
      Praise ye the Lord.

3 I find him present everywhere,
  Sing hallelujah!
I cast on him my ev'ry care,
  Praise ye the Lord.

4 He keeps me safely by his side,
  Sing hallelujah!
I take him as my guard and guide,
  Praise ye the Lord.

5 No other good do I possess,
  Sing hallelujah!
He is my constant happiness,
  Praise ye the Lord.

6 And thus I journey day by day,   .
  Sing hallelujah!
Rejoicing on my heavenward way,
  Praise ye the Lord.
                        G. E. Lovelight.

94   ONE BY ONE.

1 One by one we cross the river,
  One by one we're passing o'er;
One by one the crowns are given
  On the bright and happy shore.
Youth and childhood oft are passing
  O'er the dark and rolling tide,
And the blessèd Holy Spirit
  Is the dying Christian's guide;
And the loving, gentle Spirit
  Bears them o'er the rolling tide.

2 One by one we come to Jesus,
  As we heed his gentle voice;
One by one his vineyard enter,
  There to labor and rejoice.

91

One by one sweet flowers we gather
In the glorious work of love,
Garlands for the blessèd Saviour
Gather from the realms above;
And the loving, gentle Spirit
Bears them to our home of love.

3 One by one the heavy laden
Sink beneath the noontide sun,
And the aged pilgrim welcomes
Ev'ning shadows as they come;
One by one, with sins forgiven,
May we stand upon the shore,
Waiting till the blessèd Spirit
Takes our hand and guides us o'er;
And the loving, gentle Spirit
Leads us to the shining shore.

Adapted from Mrs. Lydia Baxter

95 THE SCARLET LINE.

1 THE blood of the Saviour for sinners
was shed,
In love and compassion divine;
And now through the mercy of him
who has bled
We follow the scarlet line.
Our lives are protected with Passover
blood,
Our walls with his covenants shine;
While Mercy and Pardon forever have
stood
In love by the scarlet line.

2 When Christ was uplifted, and mortals
were shown
Jehovah's far reaching design,

How Justice and Mercy were called to
    his throne,
And bound by the scarlet line,
Then hope came to earth with a heart-
    cheering word,
And sung of this life-giving sign;
And Faith quickly shouted her triumph
    in God,
That came through the scarlet line.

3 No more will the altars of victims
    arise,
Or flames from the offerings shine;
For life from the Lord has come down
    from the skies,
That ran through the scarlet line.
O holy, compassionate Lamb that was
    slain,
We live in this blessing of thine,
And, bound by the cords that forever
    remain,
We trust in the scarlet line.
                Rev. John. O. Foster, B.D.

96   THE UNCLOUDED DAY.

1 O THEY tell me of a home far beyond
    the skies,
O they tell me of a home far away;
O they tell me of a home where no
    storm-clouds rise,
O they tell me of an unclouded day;
O the land of cloudless day,
O the land of an unclouded sky;
O they tell me of a home where no
    storm clouds rise,
O they tell me of an unclouded day.

2 O they tell me of a home where my
  friends have gone,
  O they tell me of that land far away;
Where the tree of life in eternal bloom
  Sheds its fragrance through the un-
    clouded day;
  O the land of cloudless day,
  O the land of an unclouded sky;
  O they tell me of my friends by the
    tree of life,
  In the land of an unclouded day.

3 O they tell me of the King in his beau-
  ty there,
  And they tell that mine eyes shall
    behold
Where he sits on the throne that is
  whiter than snow,
  In the city that is made of gold;
  O that land mine eyes shall see,
  O that land of an unclouded sky;
  O they tell me of the King in his snow-
    white throne,
  In the land of the unclouded day.

4 O they tell me that he smiles on his
  children there,
  And his smile drives their sorrows
    all away;
And they tell me that no tears ever
  come again;
  In that lovely land of unclouded day;
  O that land of lovely smiles,
  O the smiles of his love-beaming eye;
  O the King in his beauty invites me
    there,
  To the land of the unclouded day.
                    Rev. J. K. Alwood.

97   Whosoever.

1 I PRAISE the Lord that one like me
  For mercy may to Jesus flee;
  He says that "whosoever will"
  May seek and find salvation still.

Chorus.

My Saviour's promise faileth never;
He counts me in the "whosoever."

2 I was to sin a wretchèd slave,
  But Jesus died my soul to save;
  He says that "whosoever will"
  May seek and find salvation still.

3 I look by faith and see this word,
  Stamped with the blood of Christ my
    Lord,
  He says that "whosoever will"
  May seek and find salvation still.

4 I now believe he saves my soul,
  His precious blood hath made me whole;
  He says that "whosoever will"
  May seek and find salvation still
            James Nicholson.

98

I Will Shout His Praise in Glory.

1 You ask what makes me happy, my
    heart so free from care,
  It is because my Saviour in mercy heard
    my prayer;
  He brought me out of darkness, and now
    the light I see;
  O blessèd, loving Saviour! to him the
    praise shall be.

Chorus.

I will shout his praise in glory,
   And we'll all sing hallelujah in heav-
      en by and by;
I will shout his praise in glory,
   And we'll all sing hallelujah in heav-
      en by and by.

2 I was a friendless wanderer till Jesus
      took me in;
   My life was full of sorrow, my heart was
      full of sin;
   But when the blood so precious spoke
      pardon to my soul;
   O blissful, blissful moment! 'twas joy
      beyond control.

3 I wish that ev'ry sinner before his
      throne would bow;
   He waits to bid them welcome, he longs
      to bless them now;
   If they but knew the rapture that in his
      love I see,
   They'd come and shout salvation, and
      sing his praise with me.

4 I mean to live for Jesus while here on
      earth I stay,
   And when his voice shall call me to
      realms of endless day,
   As one by one we gather, rejoicing on
      the shore,
   We'll shout his praise in glory, and sing
      for evermore.

                              P. H. Dingman.

99

Have You Something Good to Tell?

1 Have you something good to tell us,
  My Christian friend to-day?
Tell how the Lord has met you,
  And helped you on your way.

Chorus.

Tell of the loving Saviour
  Who keeps us day by day;
O tell of the precious Saviour—
  'Twill help us on our way.

2 Have you something good to tell us
  Of Jesus kind and true?
Of hopes that reach to heaven?
  Of mercies ever new?

3 We are waiting now to hear you
  Proclaim his grace so free;
Speak out and tell each sinner
  "His love has pardoned me."
                          Priscilla J. Owens

100 The Whole Wide World.

1 The whole wide world for Jesus,
  This shall our watch-word be,
Upon the highest mountain,
  Down by the widest sea.
The whole wide world for Jesus,
  To him all men shall bow,
In city or on prairie,
  The world for Jesus now.

Chorus.

The whole wide world, the whole wide
world,
Proclaim the gospel tidings through the
whole wide world,
Lift up the cross for Jesus, his banner be
unfurled,
Till ev'ry tongue confess him, through
the whole wide world.

2 The whole wide world for Jesus
Inspires us with the thought
That ev'ry son of Adam
Hath by the blood been bought.
The whole wide world for Jesus,
O faint not by the way!
The cross shall surely conquer
In this our glorious day.

3 The whole wide world for Jesus,
The marching order sound,
Go ye and preach the gospel
Wherever man is found.
The whole wide world for Jesus,
Our banner is unfurled,
We battle now for Jesus,
And faith demands the world.

4 The whole wide world for Jesus,
In the Father's home above
Are many wondrous mansions,
Mansions of light and love.
The whole wide world for Jesus,
. Ride forth, O conquering king,
Through all the mighty nations,
The world to glory bring.

Rev. J. Demster Hammond.

101 ETERNITY!—WHERE?

1 "ETERNITY!—where!" It floats in the
air;
Amid clamor or silence it ever is there!
The question so solemn—"Eternity!—
where?"
The question so solemn—"Eternity!—
where?"

2 "Eternity! — where?" O Eternity—
where?
With redeemed ones in glory? or fiends
in despair?
With one or the other!—"Eternity—
where?"
With one or the other—"Eternity!—
where?"

3 "Eternity!—where?" O how can you
share
The world's giddy pleasures, or heed-
lessly dare
Do aught till you settle—"Eternity!—
where?"
Do aught till you settle—"Eternity!—
where?"

4 "Eternity!—where?" O friend, have a
care;
Soon God will no longer his judgment
forbear;
This day may decide your "Eternity!—
where?"
This day may decide your "Eternity!—
where?"

5 " Eternity !— where?"   O Eternity! —
   where?"
   Friend, sleep not nor take in the world
   any share,
   Till you answer this question—" Eterni·
   ty! –where?"
   Till you answer this question—" Eterni·
   ty!—where?"

102

SING, O SING THE LOVE OF JESUS.

1 SING, O sing the love of Jesus,
   Boundless, deep, unmeasured love;
Let the soul-inspiring chorus
   Ring through all the courts above.

Chorus.

Sing, O sing the love of Jesus,
   Heav'n and earth repeat the strain,
Sing. O sing, till ev'ry nation
   Echoes on the sweet refrain.

2 Sing, O sing the love of Jesus,
   Render hearty thanks and praise;
While he gives us life and being,
   Praise him on through endless days.

3 Angel lips will join our anthem,
   Through the sky the sound prolong;
Heav'nly hosts take up the chorus,
   And with rapture swell the song.

4 Pow'r and might and bliss eternal
   Now and evermore shall be
Unto him who loved and saved us
   With a love so full and free.
                              May Clifton.

103 The Beautiful Land.

1 There's a beautiful land far beyond the
sky,
And Jesus my Saviour is there;
He has gone to prepare me a home on
high—
O I long, O I long to be there!

Chorus.

In that beautiful land
Where the angels stand,
We shall meet, we shall meet,
We shall meet in that beautiful land.

2 I have friends who have gone to that
land on high,
They are free from all sorrow and
care;
And I trust I shall meet them above the
sky—
O I long, O I long to be there!

3 We shall meet in that beautiful land on
high,
And be with the bright and the fair;
Where the waters of life sweetly mur-
mur by—
O I long, O I long to be there!

104 Abiding and Confiding.

1 I have learned the wondrous secret
Of abiding in the Lord;
I have found the strength and sweetness
Of confiding in his word;

101

I have tasted life's pure fountain,
  I am drinking of his blood,
I have lost myself in Jesus,
  I am sinking into God.

Chorus.

I'm abiding in the Lord,
  And confiding in his word,
And I'm hiding, safely hiding,
  In the bosom of his love.

2 I am crucified with Jesus,
    And he lives and dwells in me;
  I have ceased from all my struggling,
    'Tis no longer I, but he;
  All my will is yielded to him,
    And his Spirit reigns within,
  And his precious blood each moment
    Keeps me cleansed and free from sin.

3 All my sicknesses I bring him,
    And he bears them all away;
  All my fears and griefs I tell him,
    All my cares from day to day.
  All my strength I draw from Jesus,
    By his breath I live and move;
  E'en his very mind he gives me,
    And his faith and life and love.

4 For my words I take his wisdom,
    For my works, his Spirit's power;
  For my ways, his gracious Presence
    Guards and guides me ev'ry hour.
  Of my heart he is the Portion;
    Of my joy, the ceaseless Spring;
  Saviour, Sanctifier, Healer,
    Glorious Lord and coming King!

                    Rev. A. B. Simpson.

105 ANOTHER YEAR.

1 ANOTHER year is dawning;
Dear Master, let it be,
In working or in waiting,
Another year with thee:
Another year of leaning
Upon thy loving breast,
Of ever deep'ning trustfulness,
Of quiet, happy rest.

2 Another year of mercies,
Of faithfulness and grace;
Another year of gladness
In the shining of thy face.
Another year of progress,
Another year of praise,
Another year of proving
Thy presence "all the days."

4 Another year of service,
Of witness of thy love;
Another year of training
For holier work above.
Another year is dawning,
Dear Master, let it be,
On earth or else in heaven,
Another year for thee.
Frances Ridley Havergal.

106
THERE'S A BLESSING FOR ME.

1 THERE is perfect cleansing in the precious blood
That flows for all so free,

103

There is full salvation in its crimson
   flood;
  There's a blessing from the Lord for
   me.

Chorus.

There's a blessing for me, there's a bless-
   ing for me,
A blessing from the Lord for me;
There is full salvation in the crimson
   flood:
There's a blessing from the Lord for me.

2 I am saved each moment through the
   cleansing blood
  That now by faith I see;
I am sweetly resting at the cross I love;
  There's a blessing from the Lord for
   me.

3 O the blood that keeps me from the
   power of sin
  My constant theme shall be;
I have laid my burden at the Saviour's
   feet;
  There's a blessing from the Lord for
   me.

4 There is life eternal in the precious
   blood
  That still is flowing free,
And my soul shall glory in the Saviour's
   cross;
  There's a blessing from the Lord for
   me.

Henrietta E. Blair.

107 THE BEAUTIFUL LIGHT.

1 JESUS is the light, the way,
    We are walking in the light, we are
    walking in the light;
Shining brighter day by day,
    We are walking in the beautiful light
    of God.

Refrain.

We are walking in the light,
We are walking in the light,
We are walking in the light,
We are walking in the beautiful light of
God.

2 We who know our sins forgiven,
    We are walking in the light, we are
    walking in the light—
Find on earth the joy of heaven,
    We are walking in the beautiful light
    of God.

3 As we journey here below,
    We are walking in the light, we are
    walking in the light;
O what joy and peace we know;
    We are walking in the beautiful light
    of God.

4 We will sing his power to save,
    We are walking in the light, we are
    walking in the light;
We will triumph o'er the grave;
    We are walking in the beautiful light
    of God.

R. Kelso Carter.

105

108
The Precious Love of Jesus.

1 O sing the power of love divine,
The precious love of Jesus;
That bids the light in darkness shine,
And wins the lost to Jesus.

Chorus.

O precious, pure, unchanging love—
The boundless love of Jesus—
It binds our hearts in union sweet,
And makes us one in Jesus.

2 'Tis love that conquers ev'ry fear,
The precious love of Jesus;
And now by faith has brought us near
The bleeding side of Jesus.

3 'Tis love that fills the joyful heart,
And draws it up to Jesus,
Where neither life nor death can part
The sacred bonds from Jesus.

4 When faith and hope have ceased to
shine,
And we are safe with Jesus,
We'll praise the power of love divine
That brought us home to Jesus.

Fanny J. Crosby.

109 More About Jesus.

1 More about Jesus would I know,
More of his grace to others show;
More of his saving fullness see,
More of his love who died for me.

Refrain.

More, more about Jesus,
More, more about Jesus;
More of his saving fullness see,
More of his love who died for me.

2 More about Jesus let me learn,
More of his holy will discern,
Spirit of God, my teacher be,
Showing the things of Christ to me.

3 More about Jesus; in his word,
Holding communion with my Lord,
Hearing his voice in ev'ry line,
Making each faithful saying mine.

4 More about Jesus; on his throne,
Riches in glory all his own;
More of his kingdom's sure increase;
More of his coming, Prince of Peace.
E. E. Hewitt.

110   Wondrous Glory.

1 On the mount of wondrous glory,
   Borne aloft by faith, we stand,
While we drink the crystal waters
   Flowing down from Eden's land.

Chorus.

How the heart its toil forgets,
   In the joy we there behold;
In the fullness of his love,
   That is better felt than told.

2 On the mount of wondrous glory
   Where so oft 'tis ours to be,
In the brightness of his presence,
   Christ our Lord revealed we see.

3 On the mount of wondrous glory,
　　Where he bids us come and rest,
　Jesus spreads a feast before us,
　　Making each a welcome guest.

4 If on earth our souls are honored
　　With such visions of delight,
　Who can tell our heights of rapture,
　　When our faith is lost in sight.
　　　　　　　　　　Sallie M. Smith.

111 IN SOME WAY OR OTHER.

1 IN some way or other,
　　The Lord will provide;
　It may not be my way,
　It may not be thy way,
　And yet in his own way,
　　"The Lord will provide."

Chorus.

　Then we'll trust in the Lord,
　　And he will provide;
　Then we'll trust in the Lord,
　　And he will provide.

2 At some time or other,
　　The Lord will provide;
　It may not be my time,
　It may not be thy time,
　And yet in his own time,
　　"The Lord will provide."

3 Despond then no longer,
　　The Lord will provide;
　And this be the token—
　No word he hath spoken
　Was ever yet broken—
　　"The Lord will provide."

4 March on, then, right boldly,
  The sea shall divide;
  The pathway made glorious,
  With shoutings victorious,
  We'll join in the chorus,
    "The Lord will provide."
      Mrs. M. A. W. Cooke.

112   WORDS OF JESUS.

1 "COME unto me," the Saviour said,
  "Come unto me," the Saviour said;
  "Come unto me," the Saviour said,
    "And I will give you rest."

Chorus.

O the blessèd words of Jesus!
  Precious words! hallowed words!
O the blessèd words of Jesus!
  Words of life to me.

2 I am the way, the truth, the life;
  I am the way, the truth, the life;
  I am the way, the truth, the life;
    I am the light of the world.

3 Take up the cross and follow me,
  Take up the cross and follow me,
  Take up the cross and follow me,
    And thou shalt have treasure in
      heav'n.

4 Ask and it shall be given you,
  Ask and it shall be given you,
  Ask and it shall be given you,
    Seek and ye shall find.

5 He that believeth on the Son,
  He that believeth on the Son,
  He that believeth on the Son
    Hath everlasting life.

6 Look unto me and be ye saved,
  Look unto me and be ye saved,
  Look unto me and be ye saved,
    All the ends of the earth.

7 Blessèd are the pure in heart,
  Blessèd are the pure in heart,
  Blessèd are the pure in heart,
    For they shall see God.

8 Rejoice and be exceeding glad,
  Rejoice and be exceeding glad,
  Rejoice and be exceeding glad,
    For great is your reward in heaven.

9 I will not leave you comfortless,
  I will not leave you comfortless,
  I will not leave you comfortless,
    I will come unto you.

10 If any man thirst let him come unto
     me,
   If any man thirst let him come unto
     me,
   If any man thirst let him come unto
     me,
     And drink of the water of life.

11 Suffer little children to come unto me,
   Suffer little children to come unto me,
   Suffer little children to come unto me,
     For of such is the kingdom of heaven.

110

12 I go to prepare a place for you,
I go to prepare a place for you,
I go to prepare a place for you,
In my Father's house.

E. E. Hewitt.

113 No Night Over There.

1 No·night shall be in heaven; no gath-
'ring gloom
Shall o'er that glorious landscape ever
come;
No tears shall fall in sadness o'er those
flowers
That breathe their fragrance through celestial bowers.

Chorus.

No night over there,
In the cloudless realm of day,
No night over there,
Through the ages of eternity.

2 No night shall be in heaven; forbid to
sleep,
These eyes no more their mournful
vigils keep;
Their fountains dried, their tears all
washed away,
They gaze undazzled on eternal day.

3 No night shall be in heaven, but endless
noon;
No fast declining sun, no waning moon;
But there the Lamb shall yield perpet-
ual light,
'Mid pastures green and waters ever
bright.

111

4 No night shall be in heaven; no darkᵥ
ened room,
No bed of death, nor silence of the
tomb,
But breezes ever fresh with love and
truth
Shall brace the frame with an immortal
youth.

114 A Perfect Salvation.

1 With a perfect salvation through Jesus
our Lord,
We are saved by his grace,and our faith
in his word;
'Tis a gift he has purchased—his blood
it has cost;
'Tis a light in the darkness for souls that
are lost.

Refrain.

Hear the song of rapture swelling, while
the ransomed ones are telling
Of the precious blood of Jesus, that
will cleanse from every sin;
Hear them shout the wondrous story:
there is room enough in glory,
There is room enough in glory for the
world to enter in.

2 O this perfect salvation is boundless and
free,
'Tis a pledge of God's mercy to you and
to me;
Then awake out of bondage, come forth
at its voice,
O'er a sinner returning let angels rejoice.

3 On the cold, barren mountains O why
will you roam
From the warm, loving smile of a dear
Father's home.
Are you willing to trust him? then why
not believe
That a perfect salvation you now may
receive?

4 O this perfect salvation is waiting for
you,
With a garment of praise it will clothe
you anew;
It will give you a comfort no other can
bring,
It will seal you the children and heirs of
the King.

Anna C. Storey.

115 My Home Is in Heaven.

1 My home is in heaven,
Blest city above,
Summer land of delight,
Of peace and of love;
Summer land of delight,
Of peace and of love.

2 God reigns in that city,
All glorious and fair,
And its people are pure,
No sin enters there;
And its people are pure,
No sin enters there.

3 Th' redeemed of all ages
In heaven shall meet,

And we all shall unite
To bow at his feet,
And we all shall unite
To bow at his feet.

4 Who made an atonement,
And died on the tree
To purchase salvation
For sinners like me,
To purchase salvation
For sinners like me.

5 Ah! then I shall praise him—
My Saviour and God—
Who bought my soul's pardon
With his precious blood,
Who bought my soul's pardon
With his precious blood.

L. L. Pickett.

116

ARE YOU WASHED IN THE BLOOD?

1 HAVE you been to Jesus for the cleans
ing power?
Are you washed in the blood of the
Lamb?
Are you fully trusting in his grace this
hour?
Are you washed in the blood of the
Lamb?

Chorus.

Are you washed in the blood,
In the soul-cleansing blood of the
Lamb?
Are your garments spotless? are they
white as snow?
Are you washed in the blood of the
Lamb?

114

2 Are you walking daily by the Saviour's
  side?
  Are you washed in the blood of the
    Lamb?
  Do you rest each moment in the Cruci-
    fied?
  Are you washed in the blood of the
    Lamb?

3 When the Bridegroom cometh, will your
  robes be white,
  Pure and white in the blood of the
    Lamb?
  Will your souls be ready for the man-
    sions bright,
  And be washed in the blood of the
    Lamb?

4 Lay aside the garments that are stained
  with sin,
  And be washed in the blood of the
    Lamb;
  There's a fountain flowing for the soul
    unclean,
  O be washed in the blood of the
    Lamb!

Rev. E. A. Hoffman.

117   Come, Ye Blessed.

1 When our Saviour in his glory
  With the angel host shall come,
  When in clouds from heaven descending
  He shall call his children home;
  When before him shall be gathered
  All the nations far and near,
  What a shout of joy will greet him
  When the welcome words we hear.

Chorus.

Come, ye blessèd of my Father,
Come, ye blessèd of my Father,
Inherit the kingdom prepared for you
From the foundation of the world.

2 To the well of living water
  If the thirsty we have led,
If the stranger we have sheltered,
  And the hungry we have fed,
If a weary, fainting brother
  We have tried to help and cheer,
O the rest that we shall enter
  When the welcome words we hear.

3 If we give our lives to Jesus
  And delight to do his will;
If we follow out his teaching,
  And his great commands fulfill,
If our light is seen by others,
  Like the noonday, bright and clear,
What a joyful, joyful meeting
  When the welcome words we hear.

Fanny J. Crosby.

118

There's a Great Day Coming.

1 There's a great day coming, a great day
    coming,
  There's a great day coming by and by,
When the saints and the sinners shall
    be parted right and left.
  Are you ready for that day to come?

Chorus.

Are you ready? are you ready?
  Are you ready for the judgment day?
Are you ready? are you ready
  For the judgment day?

2 There's a bright day coming, a bright
    day coming,
  There's a bright day coming by and
    by,
But its brightness shall only come to
  them that love the Lord.
Are you ready for that day to come?

3 There's a sad day coming, a sad day
    coming,
  There's a sad day coming by and by,
When the sinner shall hear his doom,
  "Depart, I know you not."
Are you ready for that day to come?
W. L. Thompson.

119   MEET IN THE MORNING.

1 WE are marching onward to the heav-
    enly land,
  To meet each other in the morning;
We are pressing forward to the golden
    strand,
  Where joy will crown us in the morn-
    ing.

Chorus.

In the morning, in the morning,
  We will gather with the faithful in
    the morning;

Where the night of sorrow shall be
    rolled away,
  And joy will crown us in the morn-
    ing.

2 We are trav'ling onward from a world
    of care,
  To meet each other in the morning;
  O the time is coming, we shall soon be
    there,
  And joy will crown us in the morn-
    ing.

3 We are trav'ling onward, and the way
    grows bright,
  We'll meet each other in the morning,
  Where our friends are waiting at the
    gate of life,
  And joy will crown us in the morning.

4 Where the hills are blooming on the
    other shore,
  We'll meet each other in the morning!
  Where the heart's deep longing will be
    felt no more,
  And joy will crown us in the morning.

5 In the boundless rapture of a Saviour's
    love,
  We'll meet each other in the morning;
  Then we'll sing his glory in the realms
    above,
  And joy will crown us in the morning.
H. E. Blair.

120   THE CITY OF LIGHT.

1 THERE'S a city of light 'mid the stars,
     we are told,
   Where they know not a sorrow or
     care;
And the gates are of pearl, and the
   streets are of gold,
And the building exceedingly fair.

Chorus.

Let us pray for each other, nor faint by
     the way,
   In this sad world of sorrow and care,
For that home is so bright, and is almost
   in sight,
   And I trust in my heart you'll go
     there.

2 Brother dear, never fear, we shall tri-
     umph at last
   If we trust in the word he has giv'n;
When our trials and toils and our weep-
     ings are past,
   We shall meet in that home up in
     heav'n.

3 Sister dear, never fear, for the Saviour is
     near,
   With his hand he will lead you along;
And the way that is dark Christ will
     graciously clear,
   And your mourning shall turn to a
     song.

4 Let us walk in the light of the gospel
     divine;
   Let us ever keep near to the cross;

Let us love, watch, and pray in our pil-
grimage here;
Let us count all things else but as loss.
A. S. Kieffer.

121   IT JUST SUITS ME.

1 WHAT a wonderful salvation!
For its length and breadth and height,
Far excel the grandest knowledge
Of the seraphim in light;
I can never, never fathom
Half its holy mystery,
But I know it is for sinners,
And it just suits me.

Chorus.

It just suits me,
It just suits me,
This wonderful salvation,
It just suits me.
It just suits me,
It just suits me,
This wonderful salvation,
It just suits me.

2 O this blessed " whosoever,"
Calling ev'ry one who will
To the sparkling, living waters,
Flowing fully, freely still;
No, I know not why he loves me,
But his blood is all my plea;
I can trust his " whosoever,"
For it just suits me.

3 Precious promises of Jesus,
Sweeping ev'ry human need!

For the grace of our Redeemer
  Must our highest thought exceed;
To the mighty, royal store-house
  Let us use the golden key,
Find the special, tender promise
  That will just suit me.

4 What a perfect, present Saviour!
  What a true and loving friend!
Can we ever praise him rightly?
  Tell how grace and glory blend?
Now the Prince of Peace is reigning,
  Overruling all I see:
So whatever lot he orders,
  May it just suit me!

E. E. Hewitt.

122

IN THE SECRET OF HIS PRESENCE.

1 In the secret of his presence
  I am kept from strife of tongues:
His pavilion is around me,
  And within are ceaseless songs!
Stormy winds his word fulfilling,
  Beat without, but cannot harm,
For the Master's voice is stilling
  Storm and tempest to a calm.

Refrain.

In the secret of his presence,
  Jesus keeps, I know not how;
In the shadow of the Highest,
  I am resting, hiding now.

2 In the secret of his presence
  All the darkness disappears;
For a sun that knows no setting,
  Throws a rainbow on my tears.
So the day grows ever lighter,
  Broad'ning to the perfect noon;
So the day grows ever brighter,
  Heav'n is coming, near and soon.

3 In the secret of his presence
  Never more can foes alarm;
In the shadow of the Highest
  I can meet them with a psalm:
For the strong pavilion hides me,
  Turns their fiery darts aside,
And I know whate'er betides me,
  I shall live because he died!

4 In the secret of his presence
  Is a sweet, unbroken rest;
Pleasures, joys, in glorious fullness,
  Making earth like Eden blest:
So my peace grows deep and deeper,
  Wid'ning as it nears the sea,
For my Saviour is my keeper,
  Keeping mine and keeping me!
  Rev. Henry Burton, M.D.

123 HEALING AT THE FOUNTAIN.

1 THERE is healing at the fountain,
  Come, behold the crimson tide,
Flowing down from Calvary's mountain,
  Where the Prince of Glory died.

Chorus.

O the fountain! blessèd, healing fount-
 ain!
 I am glad 'tis flowing free,
O the fountain! precious, cleansing
 fountain!
 Praise the Lord, it cleanseth me!

2 There is healing at the fountain,
 Come and find it, weary soul,
There your sins may all be covered;
 Jesus waits to make you whole.

3 There is healing at the fountain,
 Look to Jesus now and live,
At the cross lay down your burden;
 All your wanderings he'll forgive.

4 There is healing at the fountain,
 Precious fountain filled with blood,
Come, O come, the Saviour calls you;
 Come and plunge beneath its flood.
 Fannie J. Crosby.

124
The Lord Is Rich in Mercy.

1 O the Lord is rich in mercy,
 As his word will sweetly show,
And the fount will never fail us
 In its free and blessèd flow;
We have grieved the Holy Spirit,
 Heeding not his loving call,
Yet in bringing true contrition
 There is mercy for us all.

Chorus.

O there is mercy for all,
    Mercy for you, mercy for me;
O there is mercy for all,
    Mercy for you and me.

2 O the Lord is rich in mercy,
    As he reigns in life above,
And we know 'tis sweetly blended
    With his holy name of love;
As we all are weak and sinful,
    He will prove a friend indeed,
And his mercy, ever flowing,
    Meets our ev'ry want and need.

3 O the Lord is rich in mercy,
    As we all may see and know,
And he waits to hear us calling,
    Tender mercy to bestow;
We are prone to sin and error,
    We are prone to go astray,
Yet his mercy it will reach us,
    And will bring us home to-day.

E. A. Barnes.

125   MOMENTS OF BLESSING.

1 RICH are the moments of blessing
    Jesus my Saviour bestows;
Pure is the well of salvation
    Fresh from his mercy that flows.

Chorus.

Ever he walketh beside me;
    Brightly his sunshine appears,
Spreading a beautiful rainbow
    Over the valley of tears.

2 Rich are the moments of blessing,
    Lovely, and hallowed, and sweet,
When from my labor at noontide
    Calmly I rest at his feet.

3 Why should I ever grow weary?
    Why should I faint by the way?
Has he not promised to give me
    Strength for the toils of the day?

4 Though by the mist and the shadow
    Sometimes my sky may be dim,
Rich are the moments of blessing
    Spent in communion with him.
                Fannie J. Crosby.

126   WAITING AT THE POOL.

1 THOUSANDS stand to-day in sorrow,
    Waiting at the pool;
Saying they will wash to-morrow,
    Waiting at the pool;
Others step in left and right,
Wash their stainèd garments white,
Leaving you in sorrow's night,
    Waiting at the pool,
    Waiting, waiting, waiting at the pool.

2 Souls your filthy garments wearing,
    Waiting at the pool;
Hearts your heavy burden bearing,
    Waiting at the pool:
Can it be you never heard,
    Jesus long ago hath stirred
The waters with his mighty word,
    Waiting at the pool,
    Waiting, waiting, waiting at the pool.

3 Thousands once were standing near you,
    Waiting at the pool;
Come their voices back to cheer you,
    Waiting at the pool;
Back from Canaan's happy shore,
Sorrows past and labor o'er,
Where they stand in tears no more,
    Waiting at the pool,
      Waiting, waiting, waiting at the pool.

4 Mother leaves the son, the daughter,
    Waiting at the pool;
Calls to them across the water,
    Waiting at the pool;
You can never more embrace
Mother or behold her face,
If you keep the leper's place,
    Waiting at the pool,
      Waiting, waiting, waiting at the pool.

5 Step in boldly, death may smite you,
    Waiting at the pool;
Jesus may no more invite you,
    Waiting at the pool;
Faith is near you, take her hand,
Seek with her the better land,
And no longer doubting stand
    Waiting at the pool,
      Waiting, waiting, waiting at the pool.
        Rev. A. J. Hough.

127 'TIS SO SWEET TO TRUST IN JESUS.

1 'TIS so sweet to trust in Jesus,
    Just to take him at his word;
Just to rest upon his promise;
    Just to know, "Thus saith the Lord."

Refrain.

Jesus, Jesus, how I trust him!
　How I've proved him o'er and o'er.
Jesus, Jesus, precious Jesus!
　O for grace to trust him more!

2 O how sweet to trust in Jesus,
　Just to trust his cleansing blood;
Just in simple faith to plunge me.
　'Neath the healing, cleansing flood.

3 Yes, 'tis sweet to trust in Jesus,
　Just from sin and self to cease;
Just from Jesus simply taking
　Life and rest, and joy and peace.

4 I'm so glad I learned to trust thee,
　Precious Jesus, Saviour, Friend;
And I know that thou art with me,
　Wilt be with me to the end.
Mrs. Louis M. R. Stead.

128　　"Overcomers."

1 Who, who is he? Who, who is he?
Who, who is he that overcometh by the
　blood of the Lamb?
He that believeth and is born of God,
He that believeth and is born of God,
He that believeth and is born of God
　Shall overcome by the blood.

Refrain.

O the precious, precious blood!
O the cleansing, healing flood!
O the pow'r and the love of God,
Through the blood of the Lamb!

2 What shall he wear? What shall he
    wear?
  What shall he wear that overcometh by
    the blood of the Lamb?
  He shall be clothed in raiment white,
  He shall be clothed in raiment white,
  He shall be clothed in raiment white"
  That overcomes by the blood.

3 What shall he eat? What shall he eat?
  What shall he eat that overcometh by
    the blood of the Lamb?
  He shall eat of the tree of life,
  He shall eat of the tree of life,
  He shall eat of the tree of life
  That overcomes by the blood.

4 What shall he be? What shall he be?
  What shall he be that overcometh by
    the blood of the Lamb?
  He shall be a pillar in the temple of God,
  He shall be a pillar in the temple of God,
  He shall be a pillar in the temple of God
  That overcomes by the blood.

5 What shall he hear? What shall he
    hear?
  What shall he hear that overcometh by
    the blood of the Lamb?
  He shall hear his name confessed in
    heaven,
  He shall hear his name confessed in
    heaven,
  He shall hear his name confessed in
    heaven
  That overcomes by the blood.

6 What shall he have? What shall he
   have?
What shall he have that overcometh by
   by the blood of the Lamb?
God will give him all things and make
   him his son,
God will give him all things and make
   him his son,
God will give him all things and make
   him his son
   That overcomes by the blood.

7 Where shall he sit? Where shall he sit?
Where shall he sit that overcometh by
   the blood of the Lamb?
He shall sit with Jesus on his throne,
He shall sit with Jesus on his throne,
He shall sit with Jesus on his throne
   That overcomes by the blood.

8 What is the vict'ry? What is the vict'ry?
What is the vict'ry that overcometh by
   the blood of the Lamb?
Faith is the vict'ry that overcometh,
Faith is the vict'ry that overcometh,
Faith is the vict'ry that overcometh
   By the blood of the Lamb.
                              Wm. J. Kirkpatrick.

129 All the Way Long It Is Jesus.

1 O good old way, how sweet thou art!
   All the way long it is Jesus;
May none of us from thee depart!
   All the way long it is Jesus.

Chorus.

Jesus, Jesus,
Why all the way long it is Jesus,
Jesus, Jesus,
Why all the way long it is Jesus.

2 But may our actions always say
All the way long it is Jesus!
We're marching in the good old way;
All the way long it is Jesus.

3 This note above the rest shall swell,
All the way long it is Jesus!
That Jesus doeth all things well;
All the way long it is Jesus.

130 AT THE BEAUTIFUL GATE.

1 I THINK I should mourn o'er my sorrow-
ful fate,
If sorrow in heaven could be;
If no one should be at the beautiful gate,
There waiting and watching for me.

Chorus.

Yes, waiting and watching for me,
Yes, waiting and watching for me;
May many of those at the beautiful
gate
Be waiting and watching for me.

2 How sadly I'd feel in the heavenly state,
If sadness in heaven can be;
If no one should be at the heavenly gate,
Conducted to glory by me.

3 O Lord, I beseech thee for wisdom and
 grace,
 In winning lost souls unto thee;
That many may be in that beautiful
 place,
A crown of rejoicing to me.
Rev. J. H. Martin.

131 HE IS MY PORTION FOREVER.

1 ALL, all to Jesus, I consecrate anew,
 He is my portion forever;
Only his glory henceforth will I pursue,
 He is my portion forever.

Refrain.

Take, take the world, with all its gilded
 toys;
Take, take the world, I covet not its joys.
Mine is a wealth no moth nor rust de-
 stroys;
 Jesus my portion forever.

2 All, all to Jesus, my trusting heart can
 say,
 He is my portion forever;
Led by his mercy, I'm walking ev'ry
 day,
 He is my portion forever.

3 Though he may try me, this blessèd
 truth I know:
 He is my portion forever.
He will not leave me, his promise tells
 me so,
 He is my portion forever.

131

4 All, all to Jesus I cheerfully resign,
　　He is my portion forever;
　I have the witness that he, my Lord, is
　　　mine,
　　He is my portion forever.
　　　　　　　　　　　　　　Lizzie Edwards.

132　Marching on to Victory.

1 The temperance cause is moving on,
　　Our State and nation shall be free;
　A better day begins to dawn;
　We're marching on to victory.

Chorus.

　We're marching on, we're marching on,
　　We're marching on to victory;
　A better day begins to dawn,
　We're marching on to victory.

2 Thy kingdom come, O Lord, we pray;
　　'Tis coming soon, the world shall see;
　God save our homes, we cry to-day,
　While marching on to victory.

3 The temperance banner soon shall wave
　　From north to south, from sea to sea;
　With earnest step, ye true and brave,
　We're marching on to victory.

4 We soon shall join the glad refrain;
　　"The land we love at last is free!
　Hosanna! swell the joyful strain!"
　We're marching on to victory.

5 The crowning work will soon be done;
　　God speed the coming jubilee!
　Behold, the day is almost won!
　We're marching on to victory.
　　　　　　　　　　　　　Nathan Dun, B.D.

133

HOME TO MOTHER IN HEAVEN.

1 O FATHER, come kiss me once more,
  And watch by my bed just to-night,
Your Nettie will walk through the Valley of Death
  Ere dawn of the sweet Sabbath light.

Chorus.

O father, I'm going to mother so dear;
  I dreamed that I saw her last night;
And over the river sweet voices I hear,
  They call me to mansions of light—
Home, home, home to my mother in heaven.

2 O father, what news shall I take
  To Jesus and mother for you?
I'll tell him to send holy angels of light
  To bless and to comfort you too.

3 Our home here is lonely and dark,
  And oft we are hungry and cold;
But I shall go home to my mother to-night,
  Where pleasures are purer than gold.

4 O father, dear father, once more
  Of Jesus I pray you to think;
And when I am gone to my mother in heaven,
  O father, please give up your drink.

5 O father, dear father, once more
  Please read in my Bible and think:
"No drunkard shall enter the kingdom of heaven."
  O God, keep my father from drink!

A. S. Kieffer.

134   TOUCH NOT NOR TASTE.

1 SAY, who hath sorrow, contentions, and
     woe?
   They where the wine-cup is flowing who
     go.
   Look not upon it, a serpent its head
   Hides in the glow of the glittering red.

Refrain.

   Touch not nor taste, touch not nor taste;
   O from the adder that stingeth you
     haste!
   Tarry nor stay, tarry nor stay
   There when a serpent but hides to be-
     tray.

2 Say, who in spirit are wounded, in pain?
   They who go seeking the wine-cup again,
   Tarrying long till the sparkle is past;
   Lo! it shall sting like an adder at last.

3 Say, who is stricken until he must be
   Like as one tossed in the midst of the
     sea?
   They who are beaten and sickened and
     sore,
   They who have fallen on the wine-cup
     before.

4 What shall we tell them, O what can
     we say?
   How can we turn them from sinning
     away?
   Lovingly give them the brotherly hand,
   Tenderly helping the fallen to stand.

                     Mrs. M. B. C. Slade.

135   THE WAGES OF SIN.

1 I HAVE labored for thee, O sin,
   With energy night and day,
Now what shall I have for my reward,
   And what is my utmost pay?

Chorus.

"The wages of sin is death,"
   All that is promised, you know—
Nothing but death, eternal death,
   Bitter remorse and woe.

2 But I've given my youth and strength,
   My talents and time to thee;
I have bartered away my words of
      truth,
   And nothing remains to me.

3 I have slighted the voice of God,
   And stifled my conscience too;
I have done despite to the Spirit's power,
   In striving thy work to do.

4 I have severed the ties of earth,
   And ruined my hopes of heaven,
And only for thee I've lived and toiled,
   And now what reward is given?
                    William J. Kirkpatrick.

136   COMING HOME.

1 WE have wandered far away from our
      Father's home,
   In the dark and dreary paths of sin;
But we hear our Saviour's voice, calling
      us to come,
   And at once a better life begin.

Refrain.

We are coming home,
We are coming home, coming home to-
    day;
We have heard thy welcome voice,
Blessèd Saviour, and rejoice;
We are coming home to-day.

2 We are coming now by faith, by the
    Spirit led,
    We are coming with our hearts to
        thee;
We are trusting in the blood that for us
    was shed,
And the Holy Spirit sets us free.

3 We have kindred gone before to the
    heavenly home,
    And they draw us by the cords of
        love;
They are calling us to-day, calling us to
    come
To the happy, happy home above.

Rev. J. P. Dimmitt.

137   HE'S MIGHTY TO SAVE.

1 JESUS is waiting his grace to bestow;
    Sin, "red like crimson," he makes white
        as snow;
    Loving us freely, his life-blood he gave;
    Blessèd Redeemer! he's mighty to save.

Chorus.

Mighty to save, mighty to save,
Jesus is mighty to save;
Mighty to save, mighty to save,
Jesus is mighty to save.

2 Standing alone in the strife we shall
  fail:
  Close to our Leader, his might will pre-
  vail;
  Or, if a blessing for others we crave,
  Pray on, believing—he's mighty to save.

3 Take him the burden that weighs on
  your heart,
  Take him the trouble, he'll comfort impart;
  Held by his hand, we can walk on the
  wave;
  Look up to Jesus, he's mighty to save.

4 Up from the valley the darkness is gone
  When Jesus brings there the beauty of
  dawn;
  Vict'ry, glad vic'try, we sing o'er the
  grave!
  Glory to Jesus! he's mighty to save.
  E. E. Hewitt.

138

No Burdens Allowed to Pass Through.

1 Where deserts abundantly bloom,
  And souls full of music are found,
  Who journey along day by day,
  Tasting fruits that in Canaan abound;
  A way is cast up for our feet
  By Jesus, the faithful and true,
  And over the gate-way is always in-
  scribed:
  "No burdens allowed to pass through."

Chorus.

No burdens allowed to pass through,
No burdens, no burdens with you;
Leave all at the cross there by Calvary's
    tree,
No burdens allowed to pass through.

2 This holy and beautiful way
    No ravenous beast can pass o'er;
The foot that's unclean is debarred
      From touching that crystal - paved
      floor;
But wayfaring men shall not err
    Who keep only Jesus in view,
And read what is written, so truthful
      and clear:
      "No burdens allowed to pass through."

3 Redeemed ones, with garments made
      clean
    In blood that was shed for the lost,
Walk there with a comfort unknown
    Before they the threshhold had crossed.
Cross over! away with your fear!
    O glory! there's room there for you;
And still at the gate-way you ever will
      hear:
    ' No burdens allowed to pass through."

4 Here songs interwoven with joy
    On the heads of the ransomed abide,
While nearing the Zion above,
    Just floating on love's silv'ry tide.

Be careful for nothing, belovèd,
  For Jesus still careth for you;
See! there on the arch, wrote in letters
  of light:
  "No burdens allowed to pass through."
Abbie Mills.

139   Vale of Beulah.

1 I am passing down the valley that they
    say is so lone,
  But I find that all the pathway is with
    flowers overgrown,
  'Tis to me the vale of Beulah, 'tis a
    beautiful way,
  For the Saviour walks beside me, my
    companion all day.

Chorus.

Vale of Beulah! Vale of Beulah!
  Thou art precious to me;
For the lovely land of heaven,
  In the distance I see.

2 Not a shadow, not a shadow ever dark-
    ens the way,
  For a radiance of rare glory shines upon
    it all day:
  And the music, sweetly chanted by the
    heavenly throng,
  Floats in cadence down the valley, and
    it cheers me along.

3 So I journey with rejoicing toward the
    City of Light,
  While each day my joy is deeper and
    the path grows more bright;

139

And I near the open portals of the king-
dom above,
For this highway leads to heaven to the
Kingdom of Love.

E. A. Hoffman.

140   Glory to God, Hallelujah!

1 We are never, never weary of the grand
old song;
Glory to God, hallelujah!
We can sing it loud as ever with our
faith more strong:
Glory to God, hallelujah!

Chorus.

O the children of the Lord have a right
to shout and sing,
For the way is growing bright and our
souls are on the wing,
We are going by and by to the palace of
a King!
Glory to God, hallelujah!

2 We are lost amid the rapture of redeem-
ing love;
Glory to God, hallelujah!
We are rising on its pinions to the hills
above;
Glory to God, hallelujah!

3 We are going to a palace that is built of
gold;
Glory to God, hallelujah!
Where the King in all his splendor we
shall soon behold:
Glory to God, hallejujah!

4. There we'll shout redeeming mercy in a
glad new song;
Glory to God, hallelujah!
There we'll sing the praise of Jesus with
the blood-washed throng:
Glory to God, hallelujah!

Fanny J. Crosby.

141   Come and See.

1 THERE is pardon sweet, at the Master's
feet,
Come and see, O come and see;
There's a song of peace that shall never
cease,
Come, O come and see.

Chorus.

In the precious, precious blood of Jesus,
Washed away your sins may be;
You may plunge just now in its cleansing
flood,
Come, will you come and see?

2 There's an easy yoke that you all may
bear,
Come and see, O come and see!
There's a holy joy that you all may
share,
Come, O come and see.

3 There's a healing balm for the weary
breast,
Come and see, O come and see;
There's tranquil peace and a sacred rest,
Come, O come and see.

141

4 There's a life beyond, 'tis a life divine,
  Come and see, O come and see;
And the light of faith on your path will
    shine,
  Come, O come and see.
                          Charles H. Elliott.

142 I HAVE COME TO THE FOUNTAIN.

1 I WAS once far away from my Saviour,
  Far away from his kind, loving care;
I had injured him times without num-
    ber,
  I was down in the depths of despair.

Chorus.

I have come to the Fountain of cleans-
    ing,
  To the Fountain of cleasing from sin;
Washed and made free from all sin
    would I be,
  Just now entering in.

2 His Spirit sought out my poor refuge.
  Sent conviction and knowledge of sin,
I sought for my Lord till I found him,
  And knew that my soul was redeemed.

3 Just now I plunge into the Fountain,
  Just now I hear, "go, sin no more,"
My heart is washed clean, I will praise
    him!
  My soul as an eagle doth soar.

4 I will bless him forever and ever
  Who saved a poor rebel like me,
In life will proclaim him to others,
  And praise him eternally.
                        Rev. William M. Carr.

143 Glory to Jesus, He Saves.

1 Glory to Jesus, who died on the tree,
  Paid the great price that my soul might
    be free;
  Now I can sing hallelujah to God,
  Glory! he saves, he saves.

Chorus.

  Glory! he saves, glory! he saves,
    Saves a poor sinner like me;
  Glory! he saves, glory! he saves,
    Saves a poor sinner like me.

2 Once in my heart there was sin and de-
    spair,
  Now the dear Saviour himself dwelleth
    there,
  And from his presence comes peace to
    my soul,
  Glory! he saves, he saves.

3 Come, then, ye weary, who long to be
    free,
  Come to the Saviour, he waiteth for thee;
  Then with the ransomed this song you
    can sing,
  Glory! he saves, he saves.

P. Bilhorn.

144 Ring Out the Hallelujahs.

1 Sing the song the ransomed sing,
  Let your hallelujahs ring,
  Glory to the Lord your King;
  Ring out the hallelujahs.

Refrain.

Hallelujah!
Hallelujah!
Glory to our Lord and King;
Ring out the hallelujahs.

2 Sing the love that set you free;
Sing the song of liberty,
Sing the glory yet to be;
Ring out the hallelujahs.

3 Sing the grace that made you whole;
Sing the vict'ries of the soul,
Sing while time shall onward roll;
Ring out the hallelujahs.

4 Sing till heav'n shall catch the strain,
Hallelujah yet again,
"Love redeeming" the refrain;
Ring out the hallelujahs.

Miss Emma M. Johnston.

145   Jesus Is Good to Me.

1 I LOVE my Saviour, his heart is good,
He has loved me o'er and o'er;
He sought me wand'ring, I'm saved by
his blood,
And I love him more and more.

Chorus.

Jesus is good to me,
Jesus is good to me;
So good! so good!
Jesus is good to my soul.

2 He calls, I rise, and he maketh **me**
  whole—
  How fond his tender embrace!
He cleanses and keeps me and blesses
  my soul—
  My day the smile of his face.

3 I want to love him with all my heart,
  Though all its powers are small;
I will not keep from him any part,
  For he is worthy of all.

4 He's good to me in my sorrow's night,
  He's good in the tempest's roll;
He bringeth from darkness into light,
  With joy he filleth my soul.
  Rev. E. H. Stokes, D.D.

146   Only Believe.

1 O why should we wrestle with fears
  And doubts which the Spirit must
    grieve?
And why should we languish in sorrow
  and tears,
  When there's nothing to do but be-
    lieve?

Chorus.

Believe! believe!
Only on Jesus believe;
Salvation is waiting for you and for me,
There is nothing to do but believe.

2 His word is assurance complete;
  Thy sins and thine idols now leave;
Come, pleading his promise, and fall at
  his feet,
  Then you've nothing to do but be-
    lieve.

10   145

3 How easy the terms of his grace:
  'Tis only to ask and receive;
  The seal of his favor, the smile of his
    face
  Are for those who will only believe.
  Emma M. Johnston.

147   BLESSED ASSURANCE.

1 BLESSÈD assurance, Jesus is mine!
  O what a foretaste of glory divine!
  Heir of salvation, purchase of God,
  Born of his Spirit, washed in his blood.

Chorus.

This is my story, this is my song,
Praising my Saviour all the day long;
This is my story, this is my song,
Praising my Saviour all the day long,

2 Perfect submission, perfect delight,
  Visions of rapture now burst on my
    sight;
  Angels, descending, bring from above
  Echoes of mercy, whispers of love,

3 Perfect submission, all is at rest,
  I in my Saviour am happy and blest,
  Watching and waiting, looking above,
  Filled with his goodness, lost in his
    love.
  Fanny J. Crosby.

148   MY JESUS, I LOVE THEE.

1 My Jesus, I love thee, I know thou art
    mine,
  For thee all the follies of sin I resign;

146

My gracious Redeemer, my Saviour art
thou,
If ever I loved thee, my Jesus, 'tis now.

2 I love thee because thou hast first loved
me,
And purchased my pardon on Calvary's
tree;
I love thee for wearing the thorns on
thy brow;
If ever I loved thee, my Jesus, 'tis now.

3 I will love thee in life, I'll love thee in
death,
And praise thee as long as thou lendest
me breath;
And say, when the death-dew lies cold
on my brow,
If ever I loved thee, my Jesus, 'tis now.

4 In mansions of glory and endless de-
light,
I'll ever adore thee in heaven so bright;
I'll sing with the glittering crown on my
brow,
If ever I loved thee, my Jesus, 'tis now.
"London Hymn Book."

149

CAST THY BURDEN ON THE LORD.

1 WEARY pilgrim on life's pathway,
Struggling on beneath thy load,
Hear these words of consolation:
"Cast thy burden on the Lord."

Chorus.

Cast thy burden on the Lord,
Cast thy burden on the Lord,
And he will strengthen thee, sustain
    and comfort thee;
Cast thy burden on the Lord.

2 Are thy tired feet unsteady?
    Does thy lamp no light afford?
Is thy cross too great and heavy?
    Cast thy burden on the Lord.

3 Are the ties of friendship severed?
    Hushed the voices fondly heard?
Breaks thy heart with weight of anguish,
    Cast thy burden on the Lord.

4 Does thy heart with faintness falter?
    Does thy mind forget his word?
Does thy strength succumb to weak-
    ness?
    Cast thy burden on the Lord.

5 He will hold thee up from falling,
    He will guide thy steps aright;
He will strengthen each endeavor;
    He will keep thee by his might.
              W. J. Kirkpatrick.

150 Saved to the Uttermost.

1 Saved to the uttermost: I am the
    Lord's,
Jesus my Saviour salvation affords,
Gives me his Spirit a witness within,
Whisp'ring of pardon, and saving from
    sin.

Chorus.

Saved, saved, saved to the uttermost,
　Saved, saved by power divine;
Saved, saved, saved to the uttermost,
　Jesus the Saviour is mine.

2 Saved to the uttermost: Jesus is near,
Keeping me safely, he casteth out fear;
Trusting his promises, how I am blest!
Leaning upon him, how sweet is my
　rest!

3 Saved to the uttermost, this I can say:
"Once all was darkness, but now it is
　day."
Beautiful visions of glory I see,
Jesus in brightness revealed unto me.

4 Saved to the uttermost: cheerfully sing
Loud hallelujahs to Jesus, my King;
Ransomed and pardoned, redeemed by
　his blood,
Cleansed from unrighteousness, glory to
　God!

W. J. Kirkpatrick.

151　　Gᴏᴅ Bᴇ Wɪᴛʜ Yᴏᴜ.

1 Gᴏᴅ be with you till we meet again;
By his counsels guide, uphold you,
With his sheep securely fold you,
God be with you till we meet again.

Chorus.

Till we meet, till we meet,
Till we meet at Jesus' feet;
Till we meet, till we meet,
God be with you till we meet again.

2 God be with you till we meet again,
'Neath his wings securely hide you;
Daily manna still provide you,
God be with you till we meet again.

3 God be with you till we meet again,
When life's perils thick confound you;
Put his arms unfailing round you,
God be with you till we meet again.

4 God be with you till we meet again,
Keep love's banner floating o'er you;
Smite death's threat'ning wave be-
fore you,
God be with you till we meet again.

J. E. Rankin, D.D.

152   CHRIST IS ALL.

1 I ENTERED once a home of care,
For age and penury were there,
  Yet peace and joy withal;
I asked the lonely mother whence
Her helpless widowhood's defense,
  She told me "Christ was all."

Chorus.

Christ is all, all in all,
Yes, Christ is all in all;
Christ is all, all in all,
Yes, Christ is all in all.

2 I stood beside a dying bed,
Where lay a child with aching head,
  Waiting for Jesus' call;
I marked his smile, 'twas sweet as May,
And as his spirit passed away,
  He whispered: "Christ is all."

3 I saw the martyr at the stake;
   The flames could not his courage shake,
      Nor death his soul appall.
   I asked him whence his strength was
      giv'n,
   He looked triumphantly to heav'n,
   And answered: "Christ is all."

4 I saw the gospel herald go,
   To Afric's sand and Greenland's snow,
      To save from Satan's thrall;
   Nor home nor life he counted dear,
   'Midst wants and perils owned no fear,
   He felt that "Christ is all."

5 I dreamed that hoary time had fled,
   And earth and sea gave up their dead,
      A fire dissolved this ball;
   I saw the Church's ransomed throng,
   I heard the burden of their song,
      'Twas "Christ is all in all."

6 Then come to Christ, O come to-day,
   The Father, Son, and Spirit say;
      The Bride repeats the call,
   For he will cleanse your guilty stains,
   His love will soothe your weary pains,
      For "Christ is all in all."

153   DELAY NOT TO COME.

1 DELAY not to come to Christ!
   The moments are fleeting on,
   And ere thou art scarce aware,
   The day of thy life may be gone.

Chorus.

Delay not to come,
Delay not to come,
While Jesus invites,
Delay not, delay not to come.

2 Delay not to come to Christ!
 Thy heart will grow hard as steel,
Until, though the Saviour calls,
 Thy spirit no longer can feel.

3 Delay not to come to Christ!
 For soon it may be too late,
And thou may'st be left in sin,
 Unpardoned at sweet mercy's gate.
                              E. A. Hoffman.

154   Sunshine in the Soul.

1 There's sunshine in my soul to-day,
 More glorious and bright
Than glows in any earthly sky,
 For Jesus is my light.

Refrain.

O there's sunshine, blessèd sunshine,
 When the peaceful, happy moments
  roll;
When Jesus shows his smiling face
 There is sunshine in the soul.

2 There's music in my soul to-day,
 A carol to my King,
And Jesus, listening, can hear
 The songs I cannot sing.

3 There's spring-time in my soul to-day,
    For when the Lord is near
The dove of peace sings in my heart,
    The flowers of grace appear.

4 There's gladness in my soul to-day,
    And hope, and praise, and love,
For blessings which he gives me now,
    For joys "laid up" above.

E. E. Hewitt.

155 BREATHE UPON Us.

1 REVIVE, O Lord, our waiting souls,
    Renew our altar fire!
And every heart, for thy blest work,
    With sacred zeal inspire!

Refrain.

Come, Lord, and breathe upon us,
    With thine own soul divine,
And o'er thy waiting Church below
    In strength and glory shine!

2 Help us to consecrate ourselves
    Anew to thy dear will;
With living words and earnest deed
    Thy blessèd law fulfill!

3 O light the fires of fervid love
    Within each breast to-day,
And draw us closer now to thee,
    And bless us while we pray.

4 Imbue us with thy Spirit, Lord,
    And purify each heart;
Baptize us with the power we need;
    New life and strength impart!

Mrs. R. N. Turner. (Alt.)

156   Beautiful Robes.

1 We shall walk with him in white,
In that country pure and bright,
    Where shall enter naught that may
      defile;
Where the day-beam ne'er declines,
For the blessèd light that shines
    Is the glory of the Saviour's smile.

Chorus.

Beautiful robes, beautiful robes,
    Beautiful robes we then shall wear.
Garments of light, lovely and bright,
Walking with Jesus in white,
    Beautiful robes we shall wear.

2 We shall walk with him in white,
Where faith yields to blissful sight,
    When the beauty of the King we see;
Holding converse full and sweet,
In a fellowship complete;
    Waking songs of holy melody.

3 We shall walk with him in white,
By the fountains of delight,
    Where the Lamb his ransomed ones
      shall lead,
For his blood shall wash each stain,
Till no spot of sin remain,
    And the soul for evermore is freed.
                  E. E. Hewitt.

157   The Golden Key.

1 Prayer is the key
For the bending knee
    To open the morn's first hours;

See the incense rise
To the starry skies,
   Like perfume from the flowers.

2 Not a soul so sad,
Nor a heart so glad,
   When cometh the shades of night,
But the day-break song
Will the joy prolong,
   And some darkness turn to light.

3 Take the golden key
In your hand and see,
   As the night tide drifts away,
How its blessèd hold
Is a crown of gold
   Through the weary hours of day.

4 When the shadows fall,
And the vesper call
   Is sobbing its low refrain,
'Tis a garland sweet
To the toil-dent feet,
   And an antidote for pain.

5 Soon the year's dark door
Shall be shut no more;
   Life's tears shall be wiped away,
As the pearl gates swing,
And the gold harps ring,
   And the sun unsheathe for aye.

158   The Haven of Rest.

1 My soul in sad exile was out on life's sea,
   So burdened with sin, and distressed,
Till I heard a sweet voice saying, "Make
   me your choice;"
And I entered the "Haven of Rest!"

Chorus.

I've anchored my soul in the haven of
    rest,
  I'll sail the wide seas no more;
The tempest may sweep o'er the wild,
    stormy deep,
  In Jesus I'm safe evermore.

2 I yielded myself to his tender embrace,
  And faith taking hold of the word,
My fetters fell off, and I anchored my
    soul;
  The haven of rest is my Lord.

3 The song of my soul, since the Lord
    made me whole,
  Has been the OLD STORY so blest,
Of Jesus, who'll save whosoever will
    have
  A home in the "Haven of Rest!"

4 How precious the thought that we all
    may recline,
  Like John the belovèd and blest,
On Jesus' strong arm, where no tempest
    can harm,
  Secure in the "Haven of Rest!"

5 O come to the Saviour, he patiently
    waits
  To save by his power divine;
Come, anchor your soul in the haven of
    rest,
  And say: "My Belovèd is mine."

H. L. Gilmour.

156

159 HOME OF THE SOUL.

1 I WILL sing you a song of that beautiful
  land,
 The far away home of the soul,
Where no storms ever beat on the glit-
  tering strand,
  While the years of eternity roll,
  While the years of eternity roll;
Where no storms ever beat on that glit-
  tering strand,
  While the years of eternity roll.

2 O that home of the soul, in my visions
  and dreams
 Its bright, jasper walls I can see;
Till I fancy but thinly the veil inter-
  venes
  Between the fair city and me,
  Between the fair city and me;
Till I fancy but thinly the veil inter-
  venes
 · Between the fair city and me.

3 That unchangeable home is for you and
  for me,
 Where Jesus of Nazareth stands;
The King of all kingdoms forever is he,
  And he holdeth our crowns in his
  hands,
  And he holdeth our crowns in his
  hands;
The King of all kingdoms forever is he,
  And he holdeth our crowns in his
  hands.

4 O how sweet it will be in that beauti-
  ful land,
  So free from all sorrow and pain;
With songs on our lips, and with harps
  in our hands,
  To meet one another again,
  To meet one another again;
With songs on our lips, and with harps
  in our hands,
  To meet one another again.

Mrs. Ellen H. Gates.

160

His Blood Washes Whiter Than Snow.

1 Jesus saves me and keeps me from sin,
  By the blood that he shed on the tree;
Through his Spirit and Word I am clean,
  For his grace is abundant and free.

Refrain.

I believe Jesus saves,
And his blood washes whiter than snow;
I believe Jesus saves,
And his blood washes whiter than snow.

2 It is blessèd his presence to feel,
  And his faithful disciple to be;
For his love he delights to reveal,
  And his grace is abundant and free.

3 In his care I am happy and blest,
  And his perfect peace flows unto me,
And my spirit is always at rest,
  For his grace is abundant and free.

158

4 When in glory the Saviour we meet,
   When the King in his beauty we see,
We'll confess, as we fall at his feet,
   That his grace is abundant and free.
              Joshua Gill.

161 Jesus of Nazareth Died for Me.

1 I'm helpless Lord, to thee I fly,
   In mercy hear me when I cry,
   While now I urge one only plea:
   Jesus of Nazareth died for me.

Chorus.

Jesus of Nazareth died for me,
Died to redeem and set me free;
This is my hope, my only plea:
Jesus of Nazareth died for me.

2 I know thou wilt my sins forgive,
   For thou hast bid me turn and live,
   With longing heart I come to thee:
   Jesus of Nazareth died for me.

3 My Saviour now is lifted up,
   I look to him, my only hope,
   I trust thy word, and press the plea:
   Jesus of Nazareth died for me.

4 And now I hear thy pard'ning voice,
   That bids me in thy love rejoice,
   My soul doth triumph in the plea:
   Jesus of Nazareth died for me.
             Wm. H. Clark.

162 Jesus Is Precious to Me.

1 Sweet is the name of my Lord,
   Happy his servants must be,

Singing in joyful accord:
"Jesus is precious to me."

Chorus.

Jesus is precious to me,
Jesus is precious to me,
Saved by his grace, so full, so free,
Jesus is precious to me.

2 Precious his love that sustains,
Precious in joy and delight,
Precious in conflict and pains,
Precious in sorrow and night.

3 Precious in days of my youth,
Precious in age and decline;
Precious the voice of his truth,
Precious the hope that is mine.

4 Precious the blood that he shed,
Precious the tears that he wept;
Precious the ransom he paid,
Precious the grave where he slept.

5 Precious the cross that I bear,
Sent as a token of love;
Precious the crown I shall wear,
Radiant with glory above.
Priscilla J. Owens.

163 TAKE HOLD, HOLD ON.

1 O TURN not back in the Christian race
Till the prize is won we know;
Reach up to Christ for abounding grace,
Take hold and never let go!

Chorus.

Take hold, hold on,
Hold fast and never let go!
No matter how the wind in the tempest
    may blow,
Take hold and never let go!

2 O turn not back on life's battle-field,
    Though the world's a mighty foe;
God's arms are round thee as a shield,
    Take hold and never let go!

3 Truth's anchor firmly, surely clasp,
    As the billows near thee flow,
God's hand will close o'er thy feeble
    grasp,
    Take old and never let go!

4 Though danger threatens or d e a t h
    alarms,
    In each rising flood of woe,
Still cling to God's everlasting arms,
    Take hold and never let go!
                        Priscilla J. Owens.

164

PRAISE THE LORD FOR HIS LOVE TO ME.

1 ON the cold, barren hills I had wandered
    afar,
    I was weary as weary could be,
When the kind, loving voice of the Sav-
    iour I heard,
    And I knew he was seeking for me.

Refrain.

Praise the Lord, praise the Lord;
O my soul, rejoice and sing;
Praise the Lord for his love to me.
He redeemed me with his blood,
O the precious, cleansing flood;
Hallelujah! praise the Lord.

2 O the depths of his love that my sin
   could remove
   When so long I had turned from his
   call!
   But my guilt I confessed, for my heart
   was oppressed,
   And he freely forgave me for all.

3 O the joy that I feel I can never reveal:
   There is light where my pathway was
   dim;
   I was lost till he came; now, by faith in
   his name,
   I am trusting my future to him.

4 Praise the Lord, O my soul, for the work
   he has done,
   For his goodness and mercy to me,
   For the hope of a rest in the land of the
   blest,
   Where forever with him I shall be.

Henrietta E. Blair.

165
HE SAVES TO THE UTTERMOST.

1 I was once far away from the Saviour,
   And as vile as a sinner could be;

I wondered if Christ, the Redeemer,
  Would save a poor sinner like me.
I wandered on in the darkness,
  Not a ray of light could I see;
And the thought filled my heart with
    sadness,
  There's no hope for a sinner like me.

2 But there in that lonely hour
  A voice sweetly whispered to me,
Saying: "Christ the Redeemer hath
    power
  To save a poor sinner like thee."
I listened, and lo! 'twas the Saviour
  That was speaking so kind to me.
I cried: "I'm the chief of sinners;
  Thou cans't save a poor sinner like
    me."

3 I then fully trusted in Jesus,
  And O what a joy came to me!
My heart was filled with his praises,
  For he saved a poor sinner like me.
No longer in darkness I'm walking,
  For the light is shining on me,
And now unto others I'm telling
  How he saved a poor sinner like me.
                              Charles J. Butler.

166   In the Morning.

1 We are pilgrims looking home,
Sad and weary oft we roam,
  But we know 'twill all be well in the
    morning;
When, our anchor firmly cast,
Ev'ry stormy wave is past,
  And we gather safe at last in the
    morning.

Chorus.

When we all meet again in the morning,
On the sweet blooming hills in the
  morning,
Never more to say good-night in that
  sunny region bright,
When we hail the blessèd light of the
  morning.

2 O these tender broken ties,
  How they dim our aching eyes!
    But like jewels they will shine in the
      morning.
  When our victor palms we bear,
  And our robes immortal wear,
    We shall know each other there in
      the morning.

3 When our fettered souls are free,
  Far beyond the narrow sea,
    'And we hear the Saviour's voice in
      morning;
  When our golden sheaves we bring
  To the feet of Christ our King,
    What a chorus we shall sing in the
      morning!   .

4 Through our pilgrim journey here,
  Though the night is sometimes drear,
    Let us watch and persevere till the
      morning;
  Then our highest tribute raise
  For the love that crowns our days,
    And to Jesus give the praise in the
      morning.
                              Lizzie Edwards.

167 Help Just a Little.

1 Brother, for Christ's kingdom sighing,
    Help a little, help a little;
Help to save the millions dying,
    Help just a little.

Chorus.

O the wrongs that we may righten!
O the hearts that we may lighten!
O the skies that we may brighten!
Helping just a little.

2 Is thy cup made sad by trial?
    Help a little, help a little;
Sweeten it with self-denial,
    Help just a little.

3 Though no wealth to thee is given,
    Help a little, help a little;
Sacrifice is gold in heaven,
    Help just a little.

4 Let us live for one another,
    Help a little, help a little;
Help to lift each fallen brother,
    Help just a little.

5 Though thy life is pressed with sorrow,
    Help a little, help a little;
Bravely look toward God's to-morrow,
    Help just a little.
                    Rev. W. A. Spencer.

168 Leaning on Jesus.

1 Weary with walking alone,
    Long heavy laden with sin;
Toiling all night without Christ,
    Rest for my soul shall I win?

Chorus.

Leaning on Jesus,
    I walk at his side;
Leaning on Jesus,
    I trust him, my Shepherd and Guide.

2 Fearing to stand for my Lord,
    Trembling for weakness in prayer;
Yet on the bosom divine
    Losing each sorrow and fear.

3 Anxious no longer for self,
    Shrinking no longer from pain,
Leaning on Jesus alone,
    He all my care will sustain.

4 Leaning, I walk in " the way; "
    Leaning, " the truth " I shall know;
Leaning on heart-throbs of Christ,
    Safe into " life " I may go.

Rev. W. F. Crafts.

169   TRUSTING IN THE PROMISE.

1 I HAVE found repose for my weary soul,
And a harbor safe when the billows roll,
    Trusting in the promise of my Sav-
        iour;
I will fear no foe in the deadly strife,
I will bear my lot in the toil of life,
    Trusting in the promise of the Sav-
        iour;

Refrain.

Resting on his mighty arm forever,
Never from his loving heart to sever,
I will rest by grace in his strong em-
    brace,
Trusting in the promise of the Saviour.

2 I will sing my song as the days go by,
 And rejoice in hope, while I live or die,
   Trusting in the promise of the Sav-
    iour;
 I can smile at grief, and abide in pain,
 And the loss of all shall be highest gain,
   Trusting in the promise of the Sav-
    iour.

3 O the peace and joy of the life I live,
 O the strength and love only God can
   give,
   Trusting in the promise of the Sav-
    iour;
 Whosoever will may be saved to-day,
 And begin to walk in the holy way,
   Trusting in the promise of the Sav-
    iour.
                          Rev. H. B. Hartzler.

170 Beautiful Christmas.

1 O'er the hills and adown the snowy
   dells,
 As the echoes ring of the Christmas
   bells,
 Angel songs in our hearts resound again,
 Singing peace on earth and good-will to
   men!

                Chorus.

Bring pine and fir tree, weave the gar-
  lands bright;
Gladden the temple of the King to-
  night!
Christmas is here! Fill it with cheer!
Make it glorious with joy and light.

O'er the hills and adown the snowy
  dells,
As the echoes ring of the Christmas
  bells,
Angel songs in our hearts resound again,
Singing peace on earth and good-will to
  men!

2 Bring good-will to the suffering and sad;
  Speak the tender word that shall make
    them glad;
  Tell them how, o'er the hills of Bethle-
    hem
  When the angels sang, 'twas good news
    for them.

Chorus.

Bring pine and fir tree, weave the gar-
  lands bright;
Gladden the temple of the King to-
  night!
Christmas is here! Fill it with cheer!
Make it glorious with joy and light.
Bring good-will to the suffering and sad:
Speak the tender words that shall make
  them glad;
Tell them how, o'er the hills of Bethle-
  hem
When the angels sang, 'twas good news
  for them.

3 Peace on earth! bid all strife and tu-
    mult cease:
  For this night again gives the Lord his
    peace,

While our hands shall his temple beau-
tify,
Carol, glory be unto God most high.

Chorus.

Bring pine and fir tree, weave the gar-
lands bright;
Gladden the temple of the King to-
night!
Christmas is here! Fill it with cheer!
Make it glorious with joy and light.
Peace on earth! bid all strife and tu-
mult cease:
For this night again gives the Lord his
peace,
While our hands shall his temple beau-
tify,
Carol, glory be unto God most high.

4 So glad hearts on this happy Christmas
night
Bring your gifts of love, make his altar
bright,
Sing glad songs that shall sweetly sound
as when
Angels sang of peace and good-will to
men.

Chorus.

Bring pine and fir tree, weave the gar-
lands bright;
Gladden the temple of the King to-
night!
Christmas is here! Fill it with cheer!
Make it glorious with joy and light.

So glad hearts on this happy Christmas
    night
Bring your gifts of love, make his altar
    bright,
Sing glad songs that shall sweetly sound
    as when
Angels sang of peace and good-will to
    men.

Mrs. M. B. C. Slade.

171   I Am Saved.

1 I am saved, the Lord hath saved me,
    Help me shout the glorious news!
I have tasted God's salvation,
    And 'tis sweet as honeyed dews.

Chorus.

Glory, glory, hallelujah!
    I rejoice salvation came;
Glory, glory, hallelujah!
    I am saved in Jesus' name.

2 Loud I sing my exultation,
    Hoping it will reach the skies,
Keep, dear Lord, my soul forever
    Under thy protecting eyes.

3 Free salvation! glad salvation!
    Let us shout from pole to pole,
Until each diseasèd nation
    Feels that God hath made it whole.

4 When at last the days are gathered
    Into thy great judgment one,
May I find my name deep written,
    In the records of thy Son.

Mrs. S. L. Oberholtzer.

172 A Song of Trust.

1 God has given me a song, a song of
    trust,
And I sing it all day long, for sing I
    must;
    Ev'ry hour it sweeter grows,
    Fills my soul with blest repose,
Just how restful no one knows but those
    who trust.

Chorus.

Ye who trust in the Lord,
    O sing a glad refrain;
Raise your songs on high,
    His mighty love proclaim;
For his promise is sure,
    Ye shall not be put to shame,
    Ye shall never be confounded
    again:
Praise his name!

2 O I sing it on the mountain, in the
    light,
Where the radiance of God's sunshine
    makes all bright;
    All my path seems bright and clear,
    Heav'nly land seems very near;
Why, I almost then appear to walk by
    sight.

3 And I sing it in the valley dark and low,
When my heart is crushed with sorrow,
    pain, and woe;
    Then the shadows flee away,
    Like the night when dawns the day;
Trust in God brings light alway, I find
    it so.

4 When I sing it in the desert parched
    and dry,
  Living streams begin to flow, a rich sup-
    ply;
    Verdure in abundance grows,
    Deserts blossom like a rose,
  And my heart with joy o'erflows at
    God's reply.

5 For I've crossed the river Jordan, and I
    stand
  In the blessèd land of promise, Beulah
    Land:
    Trusting is like breathing here,
    Just as easy—doubt and fear
  Vanish in this atmosphere, in Beulah
    Land.

" Beulah."

173   SURRENDERED.

1 I HAVE surrendered to the Lord,
    The world no longer pleases;
  I'm yielding all to his control,
    Accepting only Jesus.

2 How tenderly he holds my hand!
    Through pastures green he leads me;
  My thirsting soul he satisfies,
    With heav'nly manna feeds me.

3 By day by night he's always near,
    Sweet joy and comfort bringing;
  O how my soul exults anew
    When praise to Jesus singing.

4 No noonday drought affects my soul,
    In Jesus I'm confiding;

O constant, sweet companionship,
   With Christ in me abiding.

5 O victory that's always sure!
   O blest emancipation!
O vanquished tempter of my soul!
   O free and full salvation!

Dr. H. L. Gilmour.

174   ARE YOU DRIFTING?

1 ARE you drifting down life's current,
   Drifting on a dang'rous tide?
Near the rapids' fearful peril
   All unconscious do ye glide?
Down the stream of sin and folly—
   Heeding not the danger near,
Drifting on in self-complacence,
   Feeling no remorse or fear?

Chorus.

Hark the voice of yonder pilot;
   Cease your drifting, seize the oar;
Make the blest, celestial harbor,
   Steer your bark for Canaan's shore.

2 Down the stream of worldly pleasure,
   Drifting, drifting evermore
Toward the great unfathomed ocean,
   Bound for yon eternal shore.
Drifting, drifting—going—whither?
   Aimless, purposeless—how vain!
To the dark and dread forever!
   What, O what have you to gain?

3 Heed, O heed the kind monition!
   Give your aimless wand'rings o'er;

Cease to seek in earth your pleasure,
  Head your bark for heav'n's bright
  shore,
Take on board the skillful pilot,
  Use the oars of faith and prayer;
Then you'll make the port of glory,
  God will guide you safely there.

Mary D. James.

175   Give Me Jesus.

1 When I'm happy, hear me sing,
  When I'm happy, hear me sing,
  When I'm happy, hear me sing:
    "Give me Jesus."

Chorus.

  Give me Jesus,
  Give me Jesus;
  You may have all the world:
  Give me Jesus.

2 When in sorrow, hear me pray,
  When in sorrow, hear me pray,
  When in sorrow, hear me pray:
    "Give me Jesus."

3 When I'm dying, hear me cry,
  When I'm dying, hear me cry,
  When I'm dying, hear me cry:
    "Give me Jesus."

4 When I'm rising, hear me shout,
  When I'm rising, hear me shout,
  When I'm rising, hear me shout:
    "Give me Jesus."

5 When in heaven, we will sing,
  When in heaven, we will sing,

When in heaven, we will sing:
"Blessèd Jesus."

Chorus.

Blessèd Jesus,
Blessèd Jesus,
By thy grace we are saved,
Blessèd Jesus.

176 HE WILL GATHER THE WHEAT.

1 WHEN Jesus shall gather the nations
  Before him at last to appear,
Then how shall we stand in the judgment,
When summoned our sentence to hear?

Chorus.

He will gather the wheat in his garner,
  But the chaff he will scatter away;
Then how shall we stand in the judgment?
  O how shall it be in that day?

2 Shall we hear, from the lips of the Saviour,
  The words, "Faithful servant, well done;"
Or, trembling with fear and with anguish,
  Be banished away from his throne?

3 He will smile when he looks on his children,
  And sees on the ransomed his seal;
He will clothe them in heav'nly beauty,
  As low at his footstool they kneel.

4 Then let us be watching and waiting,
   Our lamps burning steady and bright,
When the Bridegroom shall call to the
      wedding
   Our spirits made ready for flight.

5 Thus living with hearts fixed on Jesus
   In patience we wait for the time,
When, the days of our pilgrimage ended,
   We'll bask in his presence divine.

Harriet B. M'Keever.

177   Jesus Will Forgive.

1 Come, ye sinners, come to-day:
   Jesus will forgive you freely.
All your sins he'll wash away:
   Jesus will forgive you freely.

Chorus.

O come to-day!
Why longer stay away?
He will not say you nay:
   Jesus will forgive you freely.

2 Come unto the mercy-seat:
   Jesus will forgive you freely.
Humbly falling at his feet,
   Jesus will forgive you freely.

3 Lay your treasures up above:
   Jesus will forgive you freely.
Trust the riches of his love:
   Jesus will forgive you freely.

4 Earnestly a blessing seek:
   Jesus will forgive you freely.

Trembling sinner, faint and weak,
Jesus will forgive you freely.

5 He is able all to save:
Jesus will forgive you freely.
For your love his blood he gave:
Jesus will forgive you freely.

6 Then, ye sinners, come to-day:
Jesus will forgive you freely.
All your sins he'll wash away:
Jesus will forgive you freely.
Mrs. Loula K. Rogers.

178 Beulah Land.

1 I've reached the land of corn and wine,
And all its riches freely mine;
Here shines undimmed one blissful day,
For all my night has passed away.

Chorus.

O Beulah Land, sweet Beulah Land,
As on thy highest mount I stand,
I look away across the sea,
Where mansions are prepared for me,
And view the shining glory shore,
My heav'n, my home for evermore!

2 My Saviour comes and walks with me,
And sweet communion here have we;
He gently leads me by his hand,
For this is heaven's border land.

3 A sweet perfume upon the breeze
Is borne from ever vernal trees,
And flowers, that never fading grow
Where streams of life forever flow.

12   177

4 The zephyrs seem to float to me
  Sweet sounds of heaven's melody,
  As angels with the white-robed throng
  Join in the sweet redemption song.
        Edgar Page.

179   He Hideth My Soul.

1 A wonderful Saviour is Jesus my Lord,
    A wonderful Saviour to me,
  He hideth my soul in the cleft of the
    rock,
  Where rivers of pleasure I see.

Chorus.

  He hideth my soul in the cleft of the
    rock,
  That shadows a dry, thirsty land;
  He hideth my life in the depths of his
    love,
  And covers me there with his hand,
  And covers me there with his hand.

2 A wonderful Saviour is Jesus my Lord,
    He taketh my burden away,
  He holdeth me up, and I shall not be
    moved,
  He giveth me strength as my day.

3 With numberless blessings each moment
    he crowns,
  And filled with his fullness divine,
  I sing in my rapture: "O glory to God
  For such a Redeemer as mine!"

4 When clothed in his brightness trans-
    ported I rise
  To meet him in clouds of the sky,
His perfect salvation, his wonderful love,
  I'll shout with the millions on high.
Fanny J. Crosby.

180

I Hope to Meet You All in Glory.

1 I hope to meet you all in glory,
    When the storms of life are o'er;
  I hope to tell the dear old story,
    On the blessèd shining shore.

Chorus.

  On the shining shore,
    On the golden strand,
In my Father's home,
  In the happy land,
I hope to meet you there,
I hope to meet you there,
A crown of vict'ry wear
  In glory.

2 I hope to meet you all in glory,
    By the tree of life so fair;
  I hope to praise our dear Redeemer
    For the grace that brought me there.

3 I hope to meet you all in glory,
    Round the Saviour's throne above;
  I hope to join the ransomed army
    Singing now redeeming love.

4 I hope to meet you all in glory,
    When my work on earth is o'er;
  I hope to clasp your hands rejoicing
    On the bright eternal shore,
Emma Pitt.

181   Trusting in Jesus.

1 Trusting in Jesus, my Saviour divine,
I have the witness that still he is mine;
Great are the blessings he giveth to me:
O I am happy as mortal can be.

Chorus.

I am redeemed, I know it full well,
Saved by his grace, I with him shall
    dwell;
I am redeemed, and the child of his love,
Heir to a glorious crown above.

2 Once I was far from my Saviour and
    King,
Now he has taught me his mercy to sing;
Peace in believing he giveth to me:
O I am happy as mortal can be.

3 Trusting in Jesus, O what should I fear?
Nothing can harm me when he is so
    near!
Sweet is the promise he giveth to me:
O I am happy as mortal can be.

4 If while a stranger I journey below,
Filled with his fullness such rapture I
    know,
What will the bliss of eternity be,
When in his beauty the King I shall
    see?   *Frank Gould.*

182 and 183

When the Mists Have Cleared Away.

1 When the mists have rolled in splendor
    From the summit of the hills,

And the sunshine warm and tender,
  Falls in beauty on the rills,
We may read love's shining letter
  In the rainbow of the spray;
We shall know each other better
  When the mists have cleared away.

Refrain.

We shall know as we are known,
Never more to walk alone;
In the dawning of the morning
When the mists have cleared away,
In the dawning of the morning
When the mists have cleared away.

2 If we err in human blindness,
    And forget that we are dust;
  If we miss the law of kindness,
    When we struggle to be just,
  Snowy wings of love shall cover
    All the faults that cloud our day,
  When the weary watch is over,
    And the mists have cleared away.

3 When the mists shall rise above us,
    As our Father knows his own,
  Face to face with those that love us,
    We shall know as we are known;
  Lo! beyond the orient meadows
    Floats the golden fringe of day;
  Heart to heart we hide the shadows
    Till the mists have cleared away.
                              Annie Herbert.

184 His Anger Is Turned Away.

1 O Lord, I will praise thee;
   For though thou wast angry,
      Thine anger is turned away!
   By grace now is pardoned
   This heart that was hardened;
      From sin I am ransomed to-day.

Chorus.

   Hosanna! hosanna!
   The Lord is my banner,
      His anger is turned away!
   My chains have been riven,
   My sins all forgiven;
      O Lord, I will praise thee to-day.

2 O Lord, I will praise thee,
   Because thou hast saved me,
      And welcomed thy prodigal home:
   Thy great love abiding
   Hath healed my backsliding;
      From thee I will never more roam.

3 O Lord, I will praise thee,
   For great is thy mercy,
      To pardon transgressions like mine.
   Though summer had ended,
   Thine angels defended,
      And kept this late trophy of thine.

4 O Lord, I will praise thee,
   For though thou wast angry,
      Thine anger is turnèd away!
   Thy comforts now cheer me,
   Thy presence is near me,
      Thou lovest me freely to-day!

F. G. Burroughs.

185   Welcome for Me.

1 Like a bird on the deep, far away from
    its nest,
  I had wandered, my Saviour, from
    thee;
But thy dear loving voice called me
    home to thy breast,
  And I knew there was welcome for
    me.

Chorus.

  Welcome for me,
  Saviour, from thee;
A smile and a welcome for me:
  Now, like a dove,
  I rest in thy love,
And find a sweet refuge in thee.

2 I am safe in the ark; I have folded my
    wings,
  On the bosom of mercy divine;
I am filled with the light of thy presence
    so bright,
  And the joy that will ever be mine.

3 I am safe in the ark, and I dread not
    the storm,
  Though around me the surges may
    roll;
I will look to the skies, where the day
    never dies,
  I will sing of the joy in my soul.

Fanny J. Crosby.

186 ABIDING IN HIM.

1 ABIDING, O so wondrous sweet!
I'm resting at the Saviour's feet;
I trust in him, I'm satisfied,
I'm resting in the Crucified!

Chorus.

Abiding, abiding,
O so wondrous sweet!
I'm resting, resting,
At the Saviour's feet.

2 He speaks, and by his word is giv'n
His peace, a rich foretaste of heav'n!
Not as the world he peace doth give,
'Tis through this hope my soul shall
live.

3 I live; not I; through him alone
By whom the mighty work is done:
Dead to myself, alive to him,
I count all loss his rest to gain.

4 Now rest, my heart, the work is done,
I'm saved through the Eternal Son!
Let all my pow'rs my soul employ,
To tell the world my peace and joy.

Charles B. J. Root.

187 WATCH AND PRAY.

1 WATCH and pray that when the Master
cometh,
If at morning, noon, or night,
He may find a lamp in ev'ry window,
Trimmed and burning, clear and
bright.

Chorus.

Watch and pray, the Lord commandeth;
  Watch and pray, 'twill not be long;
Soon he'll gather home his loved ones
  To the happy vale of song.

2 Watch and pray: the tempter may be
      near us;
  Keep the heart with jealous care,
Lest the door, a moment left unguarded,
  Evil thoughts may enter there.

3 Watch and pray, nor let us ever weary;
  Jesus watched and prayed alone:
Prayed for us when only stars beheld
      him,
  While on Olive's brow they shone.

4 Watch and pray, nor leave your post
      of duty,
  Till we hear the Bridegroom's voice;
Then, with him the marriage feast par-
      taking,
  We shall evermore rejoice.
                        Fanny J. Crosby.

188 AT THE CROSS I'LL ABIDE.

1 O JESUS, Saviour, I long to rest
  Near the cross where thou hast died;
For there is hope for the aching breast,
  At the cross I will abide.

Chorus.

  At the cross I'll abide,
  At the cross I'll abide,
  At the cross I'll abide,
  There his blood is applied;
  At the cross I am sanctified.

2 My dying Jesus, my Saviour God,
  Who hast born my guilt and sin,
Now wash me, cleanse me with thy own
    blood,
  Ever keep me pure and clean.

3 O Jesus, Saviour, now make me thine,
  Never let me stray from thee;
O wash me, cleanse me, for thou art
    mine,
  And thy love is full and free.

4 The cleansing pow'r of thy blood apply,
  All my guilt and sin remove;
O help me, while at thy cross I lie,
  Fill my soul with perfect love.

I. Baltzell.

189 HAPPY IN THE LOVE OF JESUS.

1 BRIGHT is the day-star shining for me,
  Happy in the love of Jesus;
Now from my bondage grace makes me
    free,
  Happy in the love of Jesus.

Chorus.

Praise from my full heart loudly shall
    ring,
Born of the Spirit, child of a King;
Heir to his glory, now will I sing,
  Happy in the love of Jesus.

2 He has redeemed me, I am his own,
  Happy in the love of Jesus;
Drawn by his mercy near to his throne,
  Happy in the love of Jesus.

3 How I am honored, how I am blest!
   Happy in the love of Jesus;
Under his banner sweetly I'll rest,
   Happy in the love of Jesus.

4 Firm is my anchor, steadfast and sure,
   Happy in the love of Jesus;
All things with patience I can endure,
   Happy in the love of Jesus.
Henrietta E Blair.

190   THE KINGDOM COMING.

1 FROM all the dark places
Of earth's heathen races,
   O see how the thick shadows fly!
The voice of salvation
Awakes ev'ry nation,
   "Come over and help us," they cry.

Chorus.

The kingdom is coming,
   O tell ye the story,
God's banner exalted shall be!
   The earth shall be full of his knowl-
     edge and glory,
As waters that cover the sea.

2 The sunlight is glancing
O'er armies advancing
   To conquer the kingdoms of sin;
Our Lord shall possess them,
His presence shall bless them,
   His beauty shall enter them in.

3 With shouting and singing,
And jubilant ringing,
   Their arms of rebellion cast down;

At last ev'ry nation
The Lord of salvation
  Their King and Redeemer shall crown.
Mrs. M. B. C. Slade.

191 The Half Has Never Been Told.

1 I know I love thee better, Lord,
    Than any earthly joy,
  For thou hast given me the peace
  Which nothing can destroy.

Chorus.

  The half has never yet been told,
    Of love so full and free;
  The half has never yet been told,
    The blood it cleanseth me.

2 I know that thou art nearer still
    Than any earthly throng,
  And sweeter is the thought of thee
  Than any lovely song.

3 Thou hast put gladness in my heart;
    Then well may I be glad;
  Without the secret of thy love,
    I could not but be sad.

4 O Saviour, precious Saviour mine!
    What will thy presence be
  If such a life of joy can crown
    Our walk on earth with thee?
Frances R. Havergal.

192   A Blessing in Prayer.

1 There is rest, sweet rest, at the Master's
    feet,
  There is favor now at the mercy-seat,

For atoning blood has been sprinkled
  there;
There is always a blessing, a blessing in
  prayer.

Refrain.

There's a blessing in prayer, in believing
  prayer;
When our Saviour's name to the throne
  we bear,
Then a Father's love will receive us
  there:
There is always a blessing, a blessing in
  prayer.

2 There is grace to help in our time of
  need,
For our Friend above is a friend indeed;
We may cast on him ev'ry grief and care,
There is always a blessing, a blessing in
  prayer.

3 When our songs are glad with the joys
  of life,
When our hearts are sad with its ills
  and strife,
When the powers of sin would the soul
  ensnare,
There is always a blessing, a blessing in
  prayer.

4 There is perfect peace though the wild
  waves roll;
There are gifts of love for the seeking
  soul;

189

Till we praise the Lord in his home so
  fair,
There is always a blessing, a blessing in
  prayer.

E. E. Hewitt.

193 Saviour, Blessed Saviour.

1 O the joy, the bliss divine,
    Saviour, blessèd Saviour,
  Thus to know and call thee mine,
    Saviour, blessèd Saviour.

Chorus.

  Not a sorrow, not a care,
  Thou dost all my burdens bear,
  While the constant love I share,
  Saviour, blessèd Saviour.

2 Once my path was dark as night,
    Saviour, blessèd Saviour;
  Now thy presence makes it bright,
    Saviour, blessèd Saviour.

3 Thou did'st give thy life for me,
    Saviour, blessèd Saviour;
  Now I give my all to thee,
    Saviour, blessèd Saviour.

4 Make me stronger, day by day,
    Saviour, blessèd Saviour,
  Still to run the heav'nly way,
    Saviour, blessèd Saviour.

Fanny J. Crosby.

194   Jesus, My Joy.

1 I've found a joy in sorrow,
    A secret balm for pain,
A beautiful to-morrow
    Of sunshine after rain.

Chorus.

'Tis Jesus, my portion forever,
    'Tis Jesus, the First and the Last;
A help very present in trouble,
    A shelter from ev'ry blast.

2 I've found a branch for healing
    Near ev'ry bitter spring,
A whispered promise stealing
    O'er ev'ry broken string.

3 I've found a glad hosanna
    For ev'ry woe and wail,
A handful of sweet manna,
    When grapes of Eschol fail.

4 I've found the Rock of Ages,
    When desert wells are dry;
And after weary stages,
    I've found an Elim nigh.

5 An Elim with its coolness,
    Its fountains and its shade;
A blessing in its fullness,
    When buds of promise fade.

6 O'er tears of soft contrition
    I've seen a rainbow light;
A glory and fruition,
    So near!—yet out of sight.

Mrs. J. F. Crewdson.

195   Glory, He Saves!

1 GLORY to Jesus, he saves even me!
 All my guilt nailing to Calvary's tree;
 Paid is the debt and my soul is set free,
 Glory to Jesus, he saves!

Chorus.

Glory, he saves! wondrously saves!
 Saves a poor sinner like me;
 Glory, he saves! wondrously saves!
 Glory to Jesus, he saves!

2 Wand'ring he found me afar from the
 fold,
 Perishing there in the darkness and
 cold;
 Half of his goodness can never be told,
 Glory to Jesus, he saves!

3 Safely and sweetly he keeps me each
 day,
 Gently, so gently he leads all the way;
 Answers of peace sends he down when
 I pray,
 Glory to Jesus, he saves!

4 Blessèd companionship! cheering me so!
 Sweeter and sweeter each day shall it
 grow,
 Till to be like him I joyfully go,
 Glory to Jesus, he saves!

F. A. Blackmer.

196

By the Grace of God We'll Meet.

1 Through the gates of pearl and jasper
  To the city paved with gold,
When the ransomed hosts shall enter,
  And their gracious Lord behold,
When they meet in blissful triumph
  By the tree of life so fair
Shall we join the noble army,
  And receive a welcome there.

Chorus.

By the grace of God we'll meet
In the city's golden street,
Shouting, "Glory! hallelujah!"
At the dear Redeemer's feet.

2 When the harvest work is ended,
  And the summer days are past,
When the reapers go rejoicing
  To their bright reward at last;
When the white-robed angel leads them
  To the gates of joy so fair,
Shall we join their happy number?
  Will they bid us welcome there?

3 Let us follow on with firmness,
  Keeping ever in the way
Where our blessèd Lord has taught us,
  To be faithful, watch and pray;
Then, in garments pure and spotless,
  By the tree of life so fair,
We shall sing through endless ages
  With the countless millions there.

Fanny J. Crosby.

197 Faithful Guide.

1 Holy Spirit, faithful guide,
   Ever near the Christian's side;
   Gently lead us by the hand,
   Pilgrims in a desert land;
   Weary souls fore'er rejoice,
   While they hear that sweetest voice,
   Whisp'ring softly: "Wanderer, come!
   Follow me, I'll guide thee home."

2 Ever present, truest Friend,
   Ever near thine aid to lend,
   Leave us not to doubt and fear,
   Groping on in darkness drear.
   When the storms are raging sore,
   Hearts grow faint, and hopes give o'er,
   Whisp'ring softly: "Wanderer, come!
   Follow me, I'll guide thee home."

3 When our days of toil shall cease.
   Waiting still for sweet release,
   Nothing left but heaven and prayer,
   Wond'ring if our names were there;
   Wading deep the dismal flood,
   Pleading naught but Jesus' blood;
   Whisp'ring softly: "Wanderer, come!
   Follow me, I'll guide thee home."

198

Jesus Is Strong to Deliver.

1 When in the tempest he'll hide us,
   When in the storm he'll be near;
   All the way long he will carry us on—
   Now we have nothing to fear.

Chorus.

Jesus is strong to deliver,
  Mighty to save, mighty to save!
Jesus is strong to deliver,
  Jesus is mighty to save!

2 When in my sorrow he found me,
  Found me, and bade me be whole,
Turned all my night into heavenly light,
  And from me my burden did roll.

3 Why are you doubting and fearing,
  Why are you still under sin?
Have you not found that his grace doth
    abound!
  He's mighty to save, let him in!

4 You say: "I am weak, I am helpless,
  I've tried again and again."
Well, this may be true, but it's not what
    you do,
  'Tis *he* who's the "mighty to save."

199
THE MORNING DRAWETH NIGH.

1 O RALLY round the standard
  Of Christ, our royal King;
O rally round his standard,
  And hallelujahs sing.

Chorus.

For the morning draweth nigh,
For the morning draweth nigh;
We can see it in the distance,
We shall hear it, we shall hear it by and
    by.

2 Though long and deep the shadows
   The dreary night may bring,
Our lamps are trimmed and burning,
   Our hallelujahs ring.

3 To yonder golden region
   Our faith now plumes her wing;
Our hearts with joy are bounding,
   And hallelujahs ring.

4 To him who paid our ransom,
   And took from death the sting,
Be everlasting praises,
   Let hallelujahs ring.
                        Fanny J. Crosby.

200   SOFTLY AND TENDERLY.

1 SOFTLY and tenderly Jesus is calling,
   Calling for you and for me,
See, on the portals he's waiting and
      watching,
   Watching for you and for me.

Chorus.

, Come home, come home,
   Ye who are weary, come home;
Earnestly, tenderly Jesus is calling,
   Calling, O sinner, come home!

2 Why should we tarry when Jesus is
      pleading,
   Pleading for you and for me?
Why should we linger and heed not his
      mercies,
   Mercies for you and for me?

196

3 Time is now fleeting, the moments are
    passing,
    Passing from you and from me;
Shadows are gathering, death-beds are
    coming,
    Coming for you and for me.

4 O for the wonderful love he has prom-
    ised!
    Promised for you and for me;
Though we have sinned, he has mercy
    and pardon,
    Pardon for you and for me.
                Will L. Thompson.

201   STAY NOT.

1 JESUS is waiting to save you,
    Bring him your burden of sin;
Knock at the portals of mercy,
    Jesus will welcome you in.

Chorus.

    Stay not, stay not,
        Faithful his promise and true;
    Stay not, stay not,
        Now there is pardon for you.

2 Come when the morning is brightest,
    Come in the spring-time of youth,
Come in the vigor of manhood,
    Drink at the fountain of truth.

3 Come, and the Saviour will give you
    Life and its pleasures untold,
Come, and his mercy will keep you
    Guarded and safe in his fold.

4 Come, for the moments are flying,
    Come, ere they vanish away;
Trust not the dawn of to-morrow,
    Jesus is waiting to-day.

Henrietta E. Blair.

202

PRAISE AND MAGNIFY OUR KING.

1 GREAT is the Lord, who ruleth over all!
    Wake, wake and sing, wake, wake
      and sing;
Down at his feet in adoration fall;
    Praise and magnify our King.

Chorus.

    O ye redeemed above,
    Strike, strike your harps of love,
    Hail the Bless'd One,
    Hail the Mighty One,
    Sweetly his wonders tell,
    Loudly his glory swell,
    Praise and magnify our King.

2 Great is the Lord, who spake and it was
    done;
    Wake, wake and sing, wake, wake
      and sing;
Honor and strength, dominion he has
    won;
    Praise and magnify our King.

3 Great is the Lord! O come with holy
    mirth;
    Wake, wake and sing, wake, wake
      and sing;

Come and rejoice, ye nations of the
earth;
Praise and magnify our King.

4 Great is the Lord, and holy is his name!
Wake, wake and sing, wake, wake
and sing;
Angels and men his wondrous works
proclaim;
Praise and magnify our King.
Lizzie Edwards.

203 More Like Thee.

1 Jesus, Saviour, great Example,
Pattern of all purity,
I would follow in thy foot-steps,
Daily growing more like thee.

Chorus.

More like thee, more like thee,
Saviour, this my constant prayer shall
be—
Day by day, where'er I stay—
Make me more and more like thee.

2 Lest I wander from thy pathway,
Or my feet move wearily,
Saviour, take my hand and lead me,
Keep me steadfast: more like thee.

3 When temptations fiercely lower,
And my shrinking soul would flee,
Change each weakness into power,
Keep me spotless: more like thee.

4 When around me all is darkness,
   And thy beauties none may see,
May thy beams, O glorious Brightness,
   In effulgence shine through me!

5 When death's cold, repulsive finger
   Leaves its impress on my brow,
May thy life, within me swelling,
   Keep me singing then as now.
                W. J. Kirkpatrick.

204   Treasures in Heaven.

1 There's a crown in heaven for the striving soul,
    Which the blessèd Jesus himself will
    place
On the head of each who shall faithful
   prove,
    Even unto death, in the heavenly
    race.

            Refrain.

O may that crown in heaven be mine,
And I among the angels shine!
Be thou, O Lord, my daily guide,
Let me ever in thy love abide.

2 There's a joy in heaven for the mourning soul,
    Though the tears may fall all the
    earthly night;
Yet the clouds of sadness will break
   away,
    And rejoicing come with the morning
    light.

Refrain.

O may that joy in heaven be mine,
And I among the angels shine!
Be thou, O Lord, my daily guide,
Let me ever in thy love abide.

3 There's a home in heaven for the faith-
ful soul,
In the many mansions prepared above,
Where the glorified shall forever sing
Of a Saviour's free and unbounded
love.

Refrain.

O may that home in heaven be mine,
And I among the angels shine!
Be thou, O Lord, my daily guide,
Let me ever in thy love abide.

T. C. O'Kane.

205 SHOWERS OF BLESSING.

1 HERE in thy name we are gathered,
Come and revive us, O Lord;
"There shall be showers of blessing,"
Thou hast declared in thy word.

Chorus.

O graciously hear us,
Graciously hear us, we pray;
Pour from thy windows upon us
Showers of blessing to-day.

2 O that the showers of blessing
Now on our souls may descend,
While at the footstool of mercy
Pleading thy promise we bend!

3 There shall be showers of blessing—
  Promise that never can fail;
Thou wilt regard our petition;
  Surely our faith will prevail.

4 Showers of blessing—we need them,
  Showers of blessing from thee;
Showers of blessing—O grant them;
  Thine all the glory shall be.

Jennie Garnett.

206   Until Ye Find.

1 Alas! alas! a wayward sheep
  Had wandered from the fold,
Far o'er the mountains rough and
    steep,
  Where howling tempests rolled;
The Shepherd, with a burdened mind,
Went forth the missing one to find,
  The missing one, far, far away,
The missing one to find.

Chorus.

Go seek until ye find;
Go seek until ye find;
The missing one must not be lost,
  Go seek until ye find.

2 He sought with many a footstep sore,
  From early morn till night:
Through rocky waters where torrents
    roar,
  All pathways but the right;

Then cried with sad and burdened
    mind:
"The missing one I have failed to find,
    The missing one, far, far away,
Alas! I've failed to find."

3 How long, O Lord, must I still go?
    How long search for the sheep?
They've wandered far away, I know,
    Discouraged, lo, I weep;
How long thus go, with burdened
    mind?
"Go," Jesus saith, "until ye find:
    The missing one must not be lost,
Go, seek until ye find!"

4 I've sought my friends for many a day,
    Have prayed for many a year;
Yet still they wander far away,
    O'er mountains dark and drear;
How long thus seek with burdened
    mind?
"Seek," Jesus saith, " until ye find:
    The missing one must not be lost,
Go, seek and ye shall find!"

5 Lord, at thy word I go again,
    Believing I shall find:
I listened, and a low refrain
    Came to me on the wind;
Led by the sadly joyful sound
I rushed, and, lo, the lost was found!
    Joy! joy! O blessèd joy divine!
The lost one I have found.

Chorus.

Joy! joy! the lost is found;
Joy! joy! the lost is found;
The missing one no longer lost,
The missing one is found.

Rev. E. II. Stokes, D.D,

207   CONSECRATION.

1 My body, soul, and spirit,
  Jesus I give to thee,
A consecrated offering,
  Thine evermore to be.

Refrain.

My all is on the altar,
  I'm waiting for the fire;
Waiting, waiting, waiting,
  I'm waiting for the fire.

2 O Jesus, mighty Saviour,
  I trust in thy great name,
I look for thy salvation,
  Thy promise now I claim.

3 O let the fire, descending
  Just now upon my soul,
Consume my humble offering,
  And cleanse and make me whole.

4 I'm thine, O blessèd Jesus,
  Washed by thy precious blood,
Now seal me by thy Spirit,
  A sacrifice to God.

Mrs. Mary D. James.

208   The Firm Foundation.

1 How firm a foundation, ye saints of the
      Lord,
   Is laid for your faith in his excellent
      word!
   What more can he say, than to you he
      hath said,
   To you, who for refuge to Jesus have
      fled,
   To you, who for refuge to Jesus have
      fled?

2 " Fear not, I am with thee, O be not dis-
      mayed,
   For I am thy God, I will still give thee
      aid;
   I'll strengthen thee, help thee, and cause
      thee to stand,
   Upheld by my gracious, omnipotent
      hand,
   Upheld by. my gracious, omnipotent
      hand.

3 " When through the deep waters I call
      thee to go,
   The rivers of sorrow shall not overflow;
   For I will be with thee, thy trials to bless,
   And sanctify to thee thy deepest distress,
   And sanctify to thee thy deepest distress.

4 " When through fiery trials thy path-
      way shall lie,
   My grace, all sufficient, shall be thy sup-
      ply,

The flame shall not hurt thee; I only design
Thy dross to consume and thy gold to refine,
Thy dross to consume and thy gold to refine.

5 "E'en down to old age all my people shall prove
My sovereign, eternal, unchangeable love;
And when hoary hairs shall their temples adorn,
Like lambs they shall still in my bosom be borne,
Like lambs they shall still in my bosom be borne.

6 "The soul that on Jesus still leans for repose,
I will not, I will not desert to his foes;
That soul, though all hell should endeavor to shake,
I'll never, no never, no never forsake,
I'll never, no never, no never forsake!"
George Keith.

209 LET THE BLESSED SAVIOUR IN.

1 WHO stands outside the closèd door?
  Rise and let him in.
Who is it knocking. o'er and o'er?
  Rise and let him in.

Refrain.

Let him in,
Let him in,
Let the blessèd Saviour in;
He is standing at the door,
He is knocking o'er and o'er,
Let the blessèd Saviour in.

2 It is the Saviour calls to thee,
Rise and let him in.
He will come in and sup with thee,
Rise and let him in.

3 In patient love he pleading stands,
Rise and let him in.
The nail prints still are in his hands,
Rise and let him in.

4 All night he kept his vigils true,
Rise and let him in.
Behold his locks are wet with dew;
Rise and let him in.

5 O why should he be waiting now?
Rise and let him in.
Thy Lord, with glory-circled brow,
Rise and let him in.

6 Beware, beware! undo the door;
Rise and let him in.
Lest he should leave thee evermore,
Rise and let him in.

E. E. Hewitt.

210 Ah! 'Tis the Old, Old Story.

1 Ah! 'tis the old, old story,
Tempted and led astray,
Leaving the path of duty,
Choosing the evil way,

Breaking the hearts of mothers,
 Slighting their fervent prayers,
Sowing the seed which bringeth
 Only a wealth of tares.

Chorus.

Ah! 'tis the old, old story,
Ah! tis the old, old story,
Ah! 'tis the old, old story,
 Tempted and led astray.

2 Robbing the heart of lightness,
 Losing the bloom of youth,
Dimming the eyes' glad brightness,
 Stilling the voice of truth.
Missing the pride of manhood,
 Missing a noble aim,
Gaining a shipwrecked nature,
 Gaining a sullied name.

3 But, in an old, old story,
 Full of grace divine,
There is abundant pardon,
 Even for sin like thine,
Now with a contrite spirit,
 Turn from the ways of sin,
Knock at the gate of heaven,
 Entrance thy soul shall win.

Chorus.

Yes, 'tis the old, old story,
Yes, 'tis the old, old story,
Yes, 'tis the old, old story,
 Full of grace divine.
 Mrs. C. L. Shacklock.

208

211 Jesus, I Come to Thee.

1 Jesus, I come to thee,
    Longing for rest;
Fold thou thy weary child
    Safe to thy breast.

Chorus.

Rocked on a stormy sea,
O be not far from me,
Lord, let me cling to thee,
    Only to thee.

2 Jesus, I come to thee.
    Hear thou my cry;
Save, or I perish, Lord,
    Save or I die.

3 Now let the rolling waves
    Bend to thy will,
Say to the troubled deep,
    Peace, peace be still.

4 Swiftly the parting clouds
    Fade from my sight;
Yonder thy bow appears,
    Lovely and bright.
          Fanny J. Crosby.

212 Waiting for Me.

1 I came to the fountain that cleanseth
    from sin,
The life-giving fountain, where millions
    have been;
I came in my weakness, o'erburdened
    with care,
To find my Redeemer and Saviour was
    there.

Chorus.

Waiting for me, waiting for me,
Jesus, my Saviour, is waiting for me;
Still at the fount oft would I be,
Where Jesus, my Saviour, is waiting
   for me.

2 He saw me approaching, and tenderly
   said:
"To purchase thy ransom my blood I
   have shed,
And if thou art willing just now to believe,
The light of my Spirit thy soul shall receive."

3 I flew to his mercy, O joyful surprise!
For lo! my Redeemer had opened mine
   eyes;
I flew to the refuge no other could give,
And faithfully promised for Jesus to
   live.

4 And now in his presence I walk with
   delight,
And feel his protection by day and by
   night;
I think of the fountain, so precious and
   free,
Where Jesus, my Saviour, was waiting
   for me.

                 Frank Hendricks.

213   O Rest, Sweet Rest.

1 Thank God for a perfect salvation,
   That makes me to-day what I am;

A sanctified child of his mercy,
Redeemed by the blood of the Lamb.

Chorus.

O rest, sweet rest!
I rest in the arms of his love;
O rest, sweet rest!
I rest in the arms of his love.

2 He lifts me above the temptations
That once could allure me to sin,
He saves me from all my transgressions,
And cleanseth my spirit within.

3 I live in the constant enjoyment
Of peace that no language can tell;
Should trials in future await me,
I know with my soul 'twill be well.

4 Praise God for a perfect salvation!
My faith is unclouded and bright,
My hope, like an anchor, is steadfast,
My mansion of glory in sight.
Martha J. Lankton.

214 THE CRIMSON STREAM.

1 I STAND beside the crimson stream
That flows from Calv'ry's mount,
And long to wash away all sin,
Within its cleansing fount.

Chorus.

Now wash me, now wash me,
And cleanse me from sin;
Now wash me, now wash me,
And I shall be clean.

2 The blood of Christ alone will save
　From guilt and fear and care;
His blood will sweetly purify,
　When sought in earnest prayer.

3 I claim the promised blessing now:
　Freedom from ev'ry sin,
The power to lead a holy life,
　With Christ in God shut in.

4 I sink into the crimson stream,
　Christ's blood is now applied;
I rise again, redeemed by him,
　And wholly purified.

Chorus.

Hallelujah! hallelujah!
　I'm washed from all sin;
Hallelujah! hallelujah!
　Yes, now I am clean.
　　　　　　　Rev. W. J. Stevenson.

215　　I'M SAVED!

1 I'm saved! I'm saved! O blessèd Lord,
　I'm sweetly saved in thee;
Saved by thy blood and by thy word,
　And thine henceforth will be.

Chorus.

I'm saved! I'm saved! I'm saved!
　I'm washed in the blood of the Lamb.
I'm saved! I'm saved! I'm saved!
　I'm washed in the blood of the Lamb.

2 I'm saved! I'm saved! O joy sublime!
　I'm saved from self and sin;

I'm saved! I'm saved! O bliss divine!
And love has closed me in.

3 Saved at the cross, the blessèd cross;
   Saved without and saved within;
I'm saved! I'm saved! O what a loss
   Who fail this joy to win.

4 I'm saved! I'm saved! I'll tell it here,
   I'll sing it o'er and o'er;
I'm saved in Jesus, O how sweet!
   I'll sing it evermore.

Rev. E. H. Stokes, D.D.

216   Blessed Be the Name.

1 ALL praise to him who reigns above,
   In majesty supreme;
Who gave his son for man to die,
   That he might man redeem.

Chorus.

Blessèd be the name, blessèd be the
   name,
Blessèd be the name of the Lord;
Blessèd be the name, blessèd be the
   name,
Blessèd be the name of the Lord.

2 His name above all names shall stand,
   Exalted more and more;
At God the Father's own right hand,
   Where angel hosts adore.

3 Redeemer, Saviour, Friend of man
   Once ruined by the fall,
Thou hast devised salvation's plan,
   For thou hast died for all.

4 His name shall be the Counselor,
　The mighty Prince of Peace,
Of all earth's kingdoms Conqueror,
　Whose reign shall never cease.

5 The ransomed hosts to thee shall bring
　Their praise and homage meet;
With rapturous awe adore their King,
　And worship at his feet.

6 Then shall we know as we are known,
　And in that world above
Forever sing around the throne
　His everlasting love.

　　　　　　　　W. H. Clark.

217　　He Has Come.

1 He has come! He has come! My Re-
　deemer has come!
He has taken my heart as his own
　chosen home.
At last I have given the welcome he
　sought;
He has come, and his coming all glad-
　ness has brought.

Chorus.

He has come! He has come!
My Redeemer, my Redeemer has come,
His presence is heaven, my heart is his
　home!
My Redeemer has come!

2 He has come! He has come! My Love
　and my Lord!
Every thought of my being is swayed
　by his word.

He has come, and he reigns in the realm
  of my soul,
And his scepter is love! O blessèd control!

3 He has come! He has come! O happiest
    heart!
  He has given his word that he will not
    depart.
  What trouble can enter, what evil can
    come
  To the heart where the God of all peace
    has his home?

4 He has come to abide: and holy must be
  The place where my Lord deigns to ban-
    quet with me.
  And this is my prayer: "Lord, since
    thou art come,
  Make meet for thy presence my heart as
    thy home!"

Mrs. J. Knowles.

218

1 In a world so full of weeping,
    While the years are rolling on,
  Christian souls the watch are keeping,
    While the years are rolling on.
  While our journey we pursue,
  With the haven still in view,
  There is work for us to do,
    While the years are rolling on.

Chorus.

Are rolling on,
Are rolling on,
O the joy that we may scatter,
While the years are rolling on.

2 There's no time to waste in sighing,
While the years are rolling on;
Time is flying, souls are dying,
While the years are rolling on.
Loving words a soul may win,
From the wretched paths of sin;
We may bring the wand'rers in,
While the years are rolling on.

3 Let us strengthen one another,
While the years are rolling on;
Seek to raise a fallen brother,
While the years are rolling on.
This is work for ev'ry hand
Till, throughout creation's land,
Armies of the Lord shall stand,
While the years are rolling on.

4 Friends we love are quickly flying,
While the years are rolling on;
No more parting, no more dying,
While the years are rolling on.
In the world beyond the tomb
Sorrow never more can come,
When we meet in that blest home,
While the years are rolling on.

Harriet B. McKeever.

216

219   GRACE IS FREE.

1 THERE'S nothing like the old, old story,
    Grace is free, grace is free!
Which saints and martyrs tell in glory,
    Grace is free, grace is free!
It brought them through the flood and
    flame,
    By it they fought and overcame,
And now they cry through his dear
    name,
    Grace is free, grace is free!

Chorus.

There's nothing like the old, old story,
    Grace is free, grace is free!
Which saints and martyrs tell in glory
    Grace is free, grace is free!

2 There's only hope in trusting Jesus,
    Grace is free, grace is free!
From sin that doomed he died to free us,
    Grace is free, grace is free!
Who would not tell the story sweet
    Of love so wondrous, so complete,
And fall in rapture at his feet,
    Grace is free, grace is free!

3 From age to age the theme is telling,
    Grace is free, grace is free!
From shore to shore the strains are
    swelling,
    Grace is free, grace is free!
When that time shall cease to be,
    And faith is crowned with victory,
'Twill sound through all eternity,
    Grace is free, grace is free!
             Emma M. Johnston.

220 Abide with Me.

1 ALL the day in sweet communion,
  Jesus, I have walked with thee:
Do not now withdraw thy presence,
  From this hour abide with me.

Chorus.

Thou my life, my only guide,
  There is naught in heav'n or earth I
    ask but thee;
Hear my prayer, my soul's petition:
  Go not hence, abide with me.

2 One by one the ev'ning shadows
  Gather darkly o'er the lea,
Yet the light of peace remaineth
  If thou still abide with me.
                          Frank Gould.

221 O to Be Like Him.

1 O TO be like him,
    Tender and kind,
  Gentle in spirit,
    Lowly in mind;
  More like to Jesus,
    Day after day;
  Filled with his Spirit,
    Now and alway.

Chorus.

Yes, to be like him,
  We must abide
Near to our Saviour,
  Close to his side.

2 O to be like him,
   Quick to obey,
Child-like and truthful,
   Ready to say;
"I and my Father
   Purpose have one,
Thine, not my will,
   Ever be done."

3 O to be like him,
   Tempted in vain,
Dwelling with sinners,
   Yet without stain;
Giving our life-work
   Sinners to save,
Triumphing over
   Death and the grave.
                    Mrs. E. C. Ellsworth.

222

WHAT A GATHERING THAT WILL BE.

1 At the sounding of the trumpet, when
      the saints are gathered home,
   We will greet each other by the crys-
      tal sea,
With the friends and all the loved ones
      there awaiting us to come,
   What a gath'ring of the faithful that
      will be!

Chorus.

What a gath'ring, gath'ring,
   At the sounding of the glorious jubi-
      lee!
What a gath'ring, gath'ring,
   What a gath'ring of the faithful that
      will be!

2 When the angel of the Lord proclaims
    that time shall be no more,
      We shall gather, and the saved and
      ransomed see,
  Then to meet again together, on the
    bright celestial shore,
      What a gath'ring of the faithful that
      will be!

3 At the great and final judgment, when
    the hidden comes to light,
      When the Lord in all his glory we
      shall see;
  At the bidding of our Saviour, "Come,
    ye blessèd, to my right,"
      What a gath'ring of the faithful that
      will be!

4 When the golden harps are sounding,
    and the angel bands proclaim
      In triumphant strains the glorious
      jubilee;
  Then to meet and join to sing the song
    of Moses and the Lamb,
      What a gath'ring of the faithful that
      will be!
                  J. H. Kurzenknabe.

223   By Grace I Will.

1 WILL you go to Jesus now, dear friend?
    He is calling you to day;
  Will you seek the bright and better land,
    By " the true and living way?"

Refrain.

I will, I will! by the grace of God, I
 will;
 I will go to Jesus now;
I will heed the gospel call,
For the promise is for all;
 I will go to Jesus now.

2 Would you know the Saviour's bound-
 less love,
 And his mercy rich and free?
Will you seek the saving, cleansing
 blood,
 That was shed for you and me?

3 Will you consecrate your life to him,
 To be ever his alone?
And your loving service freely yield
 To the king upon his throne.

4 Will you follow where the Master leads,
 Choosing only his renown?
Will you daily bear the cross for him,
 Till he bids you wear the crown?
E. E. Hewitt.

224 WAIT, AND MURMUR NOT.

1 THE home where changes never come,
 Nor pain nor sorrow, toil nor care;
Yes, 'tis a bright and blessèd home;
 Who would not fain be resting there?

Chorus.

O wait, meekly wait, and murmur not,
O wait, meekly wait, and murmur not,
 O wait, O wait,
O wait, and murmur not.

2 Yet when bowed down beneath the
 load
 By heav'n allowed, thine earthly lot;
Thou yearn'st to reach that blest abode,
 Wait, meekly wait, and murmur not.

3 If in thy path some thorns are found,
 O think who bore them on his brow;
If grief thy sorrowing heart has found,
 It reached a holier than thou.

4 Toil on, nor deem, though sore it be,
 One sigh unheard, one prayer forgot;
The day of rest will dawn for thee;
 Wait, meekly wait, and murmur not.

225   A Shout in the Camp.

1 There's a shout in the camp, for the
 Lord is here,
 Hallelujah! praise his name;
To the feast of his love we again draw
 near,
 Praise, O praise his name.

Chorus.

Room for the millions! room for all!
 Hallelujah! praise his name;
Come to the banquet, great and small,
 Praise, O praise his name.

2 There's a shout in the camp like the
 shout of old,
 Hallelujah! praise his name;
For the cloud of his glory we now be-
 hold,
 Praise, O praise his name.

3 There's a shout in the ranks of the
    King of kings,
  Hallelujah! praise his name;
While we drink at the Rock from the
    living springs,
  Praise, O praise his name.

4 There's a shout in the camp while our
    souls repeat
  Hallelujah! praise his name;
There is room for the world at the Sav-
    iour's feet,
  Praise, O praise his name.
             Fanny J. Crosby.

226
Is Not This the Land of Beulah?

1 I am dwelling on the mountain,
  Where the golden sunlight gleams
O'er the land whose wondrous beauty
  Far exceeds my fondest dreams;
Where the air is pure, ethereal,
  Laden with the breath of flowers,
They are blooming by the fountain,
  'Neath the amaranthine bowers.

Chorus.

Is not this the land of Beulah,
  Blessèd, blessèd land of light,
Where the flowers bloom forever,
  And the sun is always bright?

I can see far down the mountain,
  Where I wandered weary years,

Often hindered in my journey
 By the ghosts of doubts and fears,
Broken vows and disappointments
 Thickly sprinkled all the way,
But the Spirit led, unerring,
 To the land I hold to-day.

3 I am drinking at the fountain,
 Where I ever would abide;
For I've tasted life's pure river,
 And my soul is satisfied;
There's no thirsting for life's pleasures,
 Nor adorning, rich and gay,
For I've found a richer treasure,
 One that fadeth not away.

4 Tell me not of heavy crosses,
 Nor the burdens hard to bear,
For I've found this great salvation
 Makes each burden light appear;
And I love to follow Jesus,
 Gladly counting all but dross,
Worldly honors all forsaking
 For the glory of the Cross.

5 O the Cross has wondrous glory!
 Oft I've proved this to be true;
When I'm in the way so narrow
 I can see a pathway through;
And how sweetly Jesus whispers:
 "Take the Cross, thou need'st not fear,
For I've tried this way before thee,
 And the glory lingers near."

        Anon.

227 Jesus Will Save You Now.

1 Come, O come to the ark of rest,
   Jesus will save you now;
Come with the weight of your guilt op-
   pressed,
   Jesus will save you now.

Chorus.

ome while your cheeks with tears are
   wet,
   ome ere the star of life is set,
   ome, and the step you will ne'er re-
   gret,
   Jesus will save you now.   .

Come, O come to the ark of grace,
   Jesus will save you now;
Haste to his arm and his dear embrace,
   Jesus will save you now.

3 Come, O come to the ark of love,
   Jesus will save you now;
Come, like the worn and weary dove,
   Jesus will save you now.

4 Who'll be first to arise for prayer?
   Jesus will save you now;
Who'll be the first the cross to bear?
   Jesus will save you now.
                    Henrietta E. Blair.

228   Abiding.

1 My soul for light and love had earnest
   longings,
   O how it longed for fellowship divine!
      15   225

I sought it here and there,
I sought it ev'rywhere,
    At last, through faith, the holy boon
    was mine..

Chorus.

I'm abiding, gracious Saviour,
    I'm abiding in thy precious love to-
    day;
I'm abiding, yes, abiding,
    In thy love, thy precious love, to-day.

2 O how enriching is this sacred treasure!
    Enriching to this soul, this soul of
    mine;
There's nothing anywhere
Can with this love compare,
    And I henceforth, forever, Lord, am
    thine.

3 O yes, I rest, how blessèd is the resting!
    I rest to-day, I'm resting all the time;
"Come," echoes through the air,
"Come," and the resting share,
    And Jesus will be yours as he is mine.
                              Rev. E. H. Stokes, D.D.

229   RESTING AT THE CROSS.

1 To the cross of Christ, my Saviour,
    I had brought my weary soul,
Burdened, faint, and broken-hearted,
    Praying: "Jesus, make me whole."

Chorus.

Glory, glory be to Jesus,
    I am counting all but dross,

I have found a full salvation,
I am resting at the cross;
I'm resting, I'm resting,
I'm resting at the cross.

2 At the cross, while meekly bowing,
Jesus, smiling, bade me live:
"I have died for your transgressions,
And I freely all forgive."

3 At the cross, while prostrate lying,
Jesus' blood flowed o'er my soul,
All my guilt and sin were covered,
And he whispered: "Child, be whole."

4 At the cross I'm calmly resting,
Ev'ry moment now is sweet;
I am tasting of his glory,
I am resting at his feet.
William J. Kirkpatrick.

230 REJOICING EVERMORE.

1 THOUGH troubles assail, and dangers affright,
Though friends should all fail, and foes
all unite,
Yet one thing secures us, whatever betide,
The promise assures us, the Lord will
provide.
Chorus.

Yes, I will rejoice, rejoice in the Lord;
Yes, I will rejoice, rejoice in the Lord;
Yes, I will rejoice, rejoice in the Lord;
Will joy in the God of my salvation.

2 The birds, without barn or store-house
    are fed,
  From them let us learn to trust for our
    bread;
  His saints, what is fitting, shall ne'er be
    denied
  So long as 'tis written: the Lord will
    provide.

3 When Satan appears to stop up our path,
  And fills us with fears, we triumph by
    faith;
  He cannot take from us, though oft he
    has tried,
  The heart-cheering promise: the Lord
    will provide.

4 He tells us we're weak, our hope is in
    vain;
  The good that we seek we ne'er shall
    obtain;
  But when such suggestions our graces
    have tried,
  This answers all questions: the Lord
    will provide.

5 No strength of our own, nor goodness
    we claim;
  Our trust is all thrown on Jesus' great
    name;
  In this our strong tower for safety we
    hide;
  The Lord is our power: the Lord will
    provide.

6 When life sinks apace, and death is in
    view,
  The word of his grace shall comfort us
    through:
  Not fearing or doubting, with Christ on
    our side,
  We hope to die shouting: the Lord will
    provide.

John Newton.

231   Washed White as Snow.

1 Though my sins were once like crimson
    red,
  To the healing stream my feet were led;
  In the precious blood my Saviour shed
  He washed me white as snow.

Chorus.

  O my joyful song henceforth shall be:
  'Tis the blood of Jesus cleanseth me·
  Cleanseth, cleanseth,
  O yes, it cleanseth me.

2 At the door of faith I entered in,
  And to him confessed my guilt and sin;
  With his own dear hand he washed me
    clean,
  He washed me white as snow.

3 Though my heart was all I had to give,
  Yet he smiled and bade me look and
    live;
  What a calm, sweet peace did I receive!
  He washed me white as snow.

229

4 I will sing his pow'r from death to save;
  I will sing his triumph o'er the grave;
  I will sing, while crossing death's cold
    wave,
  He washed me white as snow.
              Fanny J. Crosby.

232   BEHOLD THE BRIDEGROOM.

1 ARE you ready for the Bridegroom
  When he comes, when he comes?
  Are you ready for the Bridegroom
  When he comes, when he comes?
  Behold, he cometh! behold, he cometh!
  Be robed and ready, for the Bridegroom
    comes.

Chorus.

Behold the Bridegroom! for he comes,
  for he comes,
Behold the Bridegroom! for he comes,
  for he comes;
Behold! he cometh! behold! he cometh!
Be robed and ready, for the Bridegroom
  comes.

2 Have your lamps trimmed and burning
  When he comes, when he comes;
  Have your lamps trimmed and burning
  When he comes, when he comes;
  He quickly cometh, he quickly cometh,
  O soul, be ready when the Bridegroom
    comes.

3 We will all go out to meet him
  When he comes, when he comes;
  We will all go out to meet him
  When he comes, when he comes;

He surely cometh! he surely cometh!
We'll go to meet him when the Bridegroom comes.

4 We will chant allelúias
   When he comes, when he comes;
We will chant alleluias
   When he comes, when he comes;
Lo! now he cometh! lo! now he cometh!
Sing alleluia! for the Bridegroom comes.

R. E. Hudson.

233

WON'T YOU LOVE MY JESUS?

1 I HAVE found a friend divine,
   Won't you love him, too?
I am his and he is mine,
   Won't you love him too?

Chorus.

Won't you love my Jesus,
My precious, precious Jesus?
Won't you love my Jesus?
He is waiting now for you.

2 O how dear his name to me!
   Won't you love him too?
None can save your soul but he,
   Won't you love him too?

3 Heavy laden, care-oppressed,
   Won't you love him too?
How he longs to give you rest!
   Won't you love him too?

4 Cast your burden at his feet,
  Won't you love him too?
There is pardon pure and sweet,
  Won't you love him too?

Sallie Smith.

234   O 'Tis Wonderful.

1 In the gospel's sweet, old story,
  Lo! I read its golden theme:
How the Prince of life and glory
Came to suffer and redeem.

Chorus.

O 'tis wonderful, wonderful!
Yes, 'tis wonderful, wonderful!
O 'tis wonderful, wonderful!
The story of his love.

2 Sin its secret work was plying,
  Adding guilt with ev'ry day,
Till I read that Christ, in dying,
Died to take my guilt away.

3 To his love I was a stranger,
  To his call I gave no heed,
Till at last I saw my danger,
Found the Friend I stood in need.

E. A. Barnes.

235   Open the Door.

1 Jesus, the Saviour, is waiting and knock-
    ing,
  Standing to-day at the door of thy
    heart;

Say, wilt thou open and gladly receive
  him?
   Or wilt thou bid him in sorrow depart?   .

Chorus.

Open the door, 'tis the Saviour knocking,
   Patiently knocking to-day at thy
   heart;
Open the door, 'tis the Saviour knocking,
   Knocking, knocking; must he depart?

2 Long he has called thee, and thou hast
  refused him,
   Long he has waited thy answer to
   hear;
Still he is knocking; how canst thou be
  silent?
   Now at this moment thy doom may
   be near.

3 What if the lamp of thy life should be
  darkened?
   What if the Saviour should call thee
   no more?
Think of the anguish, thy spirit appall-
  ing,
   Knowing the day of probation is o'er.

4 While he is calling and waits to be gra-
  cious,
   Haste to admit him, the warning obey:
While he is holding the scepter of par-
  don,
   Quickly receive him; no longer delay.
                            Henrietta E. Blair.

233

236   I Am Glad.

1 I WILL tell the world around me,
How my blessèd Saviour found me,
How he broke the chains that bound me,
   And my sins he washed away;
O my grateful heart is glowing,
And with joy is overflowing;
   I will praise my dear Redeemer,
   I will praise him all the day.

Chorus.

   I am glad, I am glad, I am glad that
      Jesus found me!
With his precious blood he bought me;
   Hallelujah to his name!
I enjoy a perfect blessing,
And his constant love possessing,
   Ev'ry promise he has left me
   For myself I now can claim.

2 From the cold and barren mountain
To the precious cleansing fountain
How he led me like a shepherd,
   When my soul was far away;
To the cross I now am clinging,
And my happy song is ringing;
   I will praise my dear Redeemer,
   I will praise him all the day.

3 In his mercy I am hiding,
In his shadow still abiding;
He is teaching me with patience
   How to labor, watch, and pray.
I am trusting and believing,

I am asking and receiving;
 I will praise my dear Redeemer,
 I will praise him all the day.
Lizzie Edwards.

237   AWAY TO JESUS.

1 A LITTLE while to sow and reap,
  And then away to Jesus;
 A little while our watch to keep,
  And then away to Jesus.

Chorus.

To Jesus, to Jesus,
Away, away to Jesus,
 To feast the soul, while ages roll,
 And shout the love of Jesus.

2 A little while on earth to meet,
  And then away to Jesus;
 To feel the bliss of union sweet,
  And then away to Jesus.

3 A little while our crown to win,
  And then away to Jesus;
 A few more vict'ries over sin,
  And then away to Jesus.

4 A little while to part in tears,
  And then away to Jesus;
 A few more days, a few more years,
  And then away to Jesus.
Fanny L. Johnson.

238   GIVE ME JESUS.

1 TAKE the world, but give me Jesus,
  All its joys are but a name;
 But his love abideth ever,
  Through eternal years the same.

235

Chorus.

O the height and depth of mercy!
  O the length and breadth of love!
O the fullness of redemption,
  Pledge of endless life above.

2 Take the world, but give me Jesus,
  Sweetest comfort of my soul;
With my Saviour watching o'er me
  I can sing though billows roll.

3 Take the world, but give me Jesus,
  Let me view his constant smile;
Then throughout my pilgrim journey
  Light will cheer me all the while.

4 Take the world, but give me Jesus,
  In his cross my trust shall be;
Till with clearer, brighter vision
  Face to face my Lord I see.
               Fanny J. Crosby.

239   MY SPIRIT IS FREE.

1 I FOLLOW the footsteps of Jesus, my Lord,
  His spirit doth lead me along;
I walk in the pathway made plain by
  his word,
  And he fills all my soul with this song.

Refrain.

Glory to God, my spirit is free,
Glory to God, he purifies me;
I'm walking the thorn-path, but joy-
  ful I'll be,
While following Jesus my Lord.

2 A leper he found me, polluted by sin,
   From which he alone can set free;
He spake, in his mercy, " I will, be thou
    clean,"
   And he instantly purified me.

3 A captive in woe to my prison of night,
   The Master hath opened the door;
Shout aloud of deliverance, ye angels
    of light,
   Praise his name, O my soul, evermore.

4 Proclaim it, 'tis done, full salvation is
    wrought
   For sinners from sorrow and woe;
Sing aloud of his grace, who my pardon
    has bought,
   For his blood washes whiter than
    snow.

Rev. W. A. Spencer, D.D.

240 WONDERFUL LOVE OF JESUS.

1 IN vain in high and holy lays,
My soul her grateful voice would raise;
For who can sing the worthy praise
   Of the wonderful love of Jesus?

Chorus.

Wonderful love! wonderful love!
   Wonderful love of Jesus!
Wonderful love! wonderful love!
   Wonderful love of Jesus!

2 A joy by day, a peace by night,
In storms a calm, in darkness light;
In pain a balm, in weakness might,
   Is the wonderful love of Jesus.

3 My hope for pardon when I call,
My trust for lifting when I fall;
In life, in death, my all in all,
   Is the wonderful love of Jesus.

E. D. Mund.

241   Safe in the Glory Land.

1 In the good old way where the saints
    have gone,
  And the king leads on before us,
We are traveling home to the heavenly
    hill,
  With the day-star shining o'er us.

Chorus.

Traveling home to the mansions fair,
Crowns of rejoicing and life to wear;
O what a shout when we all get there,
  Safe in the glory land!

2 In the good old way like the ransomed
    throng,
  Unto Zion now returning,
We are traveling home at the King's
    command,
  And our lamps are trimmed and burn-
    ing.

3 In the good old way with a steadfast
    faith,
  In the bonds of love and union,
What a joy is ours for the King we see,
  And with him we hold communion.

4 Though our feet must stand on the cold,
cold brink
    Of the dark and stormy river,
With the King we'll cross to the other
side,
    And we'll sing his praise forever.
James L. Black.

242   ALWAYS ABOUNDING.

1 BE earnest, my brothers, in word and in
deed,
    Be active in reaping and sowing the
seed;
    And thus in the vineyard, with Jesus
to lead,
    Be always abounding in the work of the
Lord.

Refrain.

Be always abounding in the work of
the Lord,
Be always abounding in the work of
the Lord;
Be earnest, be active, relying on his
word,
Be always abounding in the work of
the Lord.

2 Be ready, my brothers, his call to obey,
    In seeking the erring and showing the
way;
    And thus as his servants, remember, we
pray,
    Be always abounding in the work of
the Lord.

3 Be zealous, my brothers, the light to ex-
   tend,
   And unto all nations the gospel to send;
   And thus, till the harvest in glory shall
   end,
   Be always abounding in the work of
   the Lord.

E. A. Barnes.

243 Lord, I Come Repenting.

1 Lord, I come repenting;
   Self and sin I long have sought,
   Wicked works my life has wrought,
   Sins of speech and secret thought,
   Now I come repenting.

Chorus.

Bowing low before thy throne,
Trusting in thy blood alone,
Own me, Saviour, as thine own,
While I come repenting.

2 Lord, I come believing;
   Ev'ry promise humbly claim,
   Trust the one and only Name,
   Yesterday, to-day the same,
   Now I come believing.

Chorus.

Bowing low before thy throne,
Trusting in thy blood alone,
Own me, Saviour, as thine own,
While I come believing.

3 Lord, I come obeying;
  Lo, I come to do thy will,
And, through seeming good or ill,
  Follow in thy footsteps still:
Now I come obeying.

Chorus.

Bowing low before thy throne,
Trusting in thy blood alone,
Own me, Saviour, as thine own,
While I come obeying.
Rev. Arthur T. Pierson, D.D.

244   Coming Victory.

1 THERE'S a murmur in the valley, and
    there's music on the hills,
  There's a message full of promise
    ev'rywhere;
We can read it in the sunbeams as they
    dance upon the rills,
  We can catch the floating cadence in
    the air.
Chorus.

Onward, onward now the army still ad-
  vances,
  See its banners waving in the sun;
Onward, onward now, let victory be the
  watch-word,
  The battle by the ballot must be won!

2 Lo! it whispers of the coming of a bet-
    ter, brighter day,
  And it bids us watch to see the glori-
    ous dawn;

16   241

When the mists of sin and sorrow shall
be driven far away,
As the army in its triumph marches on.

3 Hear this army's heavy footfall, how it
shakes the solid ground,
As it gathers to do battle for the right;
Hear the ringing voice of captains, and
the thrilling bugle sound,
They are calling us to muster for the
fight.

4 Soon will come a day of gladness, when
the victory we gain,
And our land, redeemed and ransomed, shall be free;
We will join the voice of millions as
they shout the glad refrain
To the welcome song of Freedom's
jubilee.

G. W. Collins.

245   I'll Be There.

1 THERE is a land of pure delight,
Where saints immortal reign;
Infinite day excludes the night,
And pleasures banish pain.

Refrain.

I'll be there, I'll be there;
When the first trumpet sounds, I'll be
there;
I'll be there, I'll be there;
When the first trumpet sounds, I'll be
there.

2 There everlasting spring abides,
    And never-with'ring flowers;
Death, like a narrow sea, divides
    This heavenly land from ours.

3 Sweet fields beyond the swelling flood
    Stand dressed in living green;
So to the Jews old Canaan stood,
    While Jordan rolled between.

4 Could we but climb where Moses stood
    And view the landscape o'er,
Not Jordan's stream, nor death's cold
    flood
Should fright us from the shore.
Isaac Watts.

246   Pray for the Fallen.

1 Pray for the fallen, O think of them
    kindly,
    Take them to Jesus, his mercy im-
    plore;
  Though they have wandered, and sad
    their condition,
    Prayer and our efforts their souls may
    restore.
Chorus.

Pray for them earnestly, pray for them
    faithfully,
    Prayers will be answered through
    Jesus' dear name;
Pray for them fervently, loving, and
    tenderly,
    Prayer and our efforts the lost may
    reclaim.

2 Pray for the fallen, O do not forsake
 them,
  Slaves to the tempter who laughs at
   their pain;
  Fast in the fetters he forged to deceive
   them,
   Pity and help them again and again.

3 Pray for the fallen, the world has re-
 nounced them!
  Keen are its glances, its censure is
   cold;
  Yet the dear Saviour will gently receive
   them,
   He will not turn them away from his
   fold.

4 Pray for the erring, O think of them
 kindly,
  They are our neighbors, though far
   they have strayed;
  They are our brothers: go forth to their
   rescue;
   Give them our friendship, our comfort, our aid.   *Martha J Lankton.*

247   THE RUM SALOON SHALL GO.

1 A wave is rolling o'er the land,
 With heavy under-tow;
 And voices sounding on the strand;
 The rum saloon shall go.

Chorus.

 Shall go, we know,
 Shall go, we know;
 A cry is sounding o'er the land,
 The rum saloon shall go.

2 Its doom is written on the sky,
   Above the shining bow;
For indignation now is high,
   The rum saloon shall go.

3 We've stood the wretched, bitter
      moans
   Full long enough, you know;
And soon we'll speak in thunder tones,
   Unless they close and go.

4 The land is tired of the curse,
   The people have said so;
And if it halts we'll make it worse,
   And help them soon to go.
                    Rev. John O. Foster, A.M.

248 Is There Any One Here?

1 Is THERE any one here that is willing to-
      day
   On Jesus the Lord to believe?
Is there any poor soul that is longing to-
      day
   The gift of his grace to receive?

Chorus.

   "Come unto me, come unto me;"
Jesus is calling, calling now to thee,
   "Come, O come unto me."

2 Is there any one here that is trying to-
      day
   The fetters of evil to break;
Any ready to follow the Saviour to-day,
   And take up the cross for his sake?

3 Is there any one here that is weary to-
day
   Or laden, or sorrow oppressed?
Is there any sad heart that is praying to-
day
   To find in the Saviour a rest?

4 Hear the Saviour's sweet voice while he
calls thee again,
   O come, and believe and obey;
He is waiting to bless, he will comfort
thee now!
   He never turned any away.
Martha J. Lankton.

249   Leading Souls to Jesus.

1 Leading souls to Jesus who are sad and
lost,
   Who upon life's waters have been tem-
pest tossed;
All the heavy laden, burdened with
their load,
   Whisp'ring of salvation through the
Lamb of God.

Chorus.

Leading souls to Jesus! O may this be
mine,
Till I cross the river to that home divine;
Sowing by all waters, till the great day
come,
When with joy the reapers shout the
harvest home.

2 Leading souls to Jesus, telling them the
way
Out of nature's darkness into God's own
day;
Kneeling with the sinner at the Saviour's feet,
Even angels cannot know of work more
sweet.

3 Leading souls to Jesus from their want
and sin,
Setting up his kingdom with its peace
within;
Till the Spirit witness within them o'er
and o'er,
Cleansed are thy transgressions: go, and
sin no more.

4 Leading souls to Jesus, as the stars to
shine,
In some humble station, Master, be it
mine;
With forgiven sinners, not alone, to
stand
When I rise to glory in the better land.
J. E. Rankin, D.D.

250 THE UNIVERSAL CALL.

1 THE Spirit and the Bride say, "Come!
And drink of the water of life."
O blessèd call,
Good news for all,
Who tire of sin and strife.

Chorus.

The Spirit says, "Come,"
The Bride says, "Come,"
And drink of the water of life;
The Spirit says, "Come,"
The Bride says, "Come,"
And drink of the water of life."

2 "O come!" let ev'ry one who hears
To all who are near him now say:
"I heard the sound,
The stream I found,
Behold the living way."

3 Whoever will, come, taste and see!
Your longings the Saviour can fill!
The stream is free
To you and me,
· And whosoever will!

Arthur T. Pierson, D.D.

251 EACH HEART THY TEMPLE.

1 THOU chief among ten thousand,
More lovely far than all,
Reveal thyself in glory,
While on thy name we call.

Chorus.

Thou chief among ten thousand,
Our only faithful Guide,
Now make each heart thy temple,
And there henceforth abide.

2 We come, as thou hast taught us,
Thy merits, Lord, we plead,
Because thou livest ever,
For us to intercede.

3 We know that thou art with us,
   We feel thy power divine;
Thy Spirit beareth witness
   That we through grace are thine.

4 Our souls and all within us,
   We consecrate to thee,
And pray that in our weakness
   Thine arm our strength may be.
                              Laura Miller.

252 Companionship with Jesus.

1 O blessed fellowship divine!
   O joy supremely sweet
Companionship with Jesus here
   Makes life with bliss replete.
In union with the purest one,
I find my heav'n on earth begun.

Chorus.

O wondrous bliss! O joy sublime!
I've Jesus with me all the time.
O wondrous bliss! O joy sublime!
I've Jesus with me all the time.

2 I'm walking close to Jesus' side,
   So close that I can hear
The softest whispers of his love,
   In fellowship so dear,
And feel his great, almighty hand
Protects me in this hostile land.

3 I'm leaning on his loving breast,
   Along life's weary way;
My path, illumined by his smiles,
   Grows brighter day by day.
No foes, no woes my heart can fear,
With my almighty Friend so near.

4 I know his shelt'ring wings of love
    Are always o'er me spread,
And though the storms may fiercely
        rage,
    All calm and free from dread,
My peaceful spirit ever sings:
    "I'll trust the covert of thy wings."
                                    Mary D. James.

253   At the Cross.

1 O Jesus, Lord, thy dying love
    Hath pierced my contrite heart;
Now take my life, and let me prove
    How dear to me thou art,

Chorus.

At the cross, at the cross, where I first
        saw the light,
    And the burden of my heart rolled
        away,
It was there by faith I received my
        sight,
    And now I am happy night and day.

2 Amid the night of sin and death
    Thy light hath filled my soul;
To me thy loving voice now saith:
    "Thy faith hath made thee whole."

3 I kiss thy feet, I clasp thy hand,
    I touch thy bleeding side;
O let me here forever stand,
    Where thou wast crucified.

4 My Lord, my light, my strength, my all,
  I count my gain but loss;
Forever let thy love enthrall,
  And keep me at the cross.

R. Kelso Carter.

254

ALL FOR ME, ALL FOR THEE.

1 SAVIOUR, I have heard thee pleading,
Passionately interceding;
Seen thy great heart broken, bleeding,
  All for me, all for me.
Lo! I come, the past lamenting,
For the wasted years repenting,
And my life henceforth presenting,
  All for thee, all for thee.

2 Thou didst stoop in thy compassion
To be found in human fashion,
And endure thy nameless passion
  All for me, all for me;
In thy name I come believing,
Of thy grace with joy receiving,
And the world behind me leaving,
  All for thee, all for thee.

3 Moved by love divine and tender,
Thou didst joyfully surrender
Palaces of rest and splendor
  All for me, all for me;
Now my soul, to life awaking,
Finds her highest joy in breaking
Bonds that bound her, and forsaking
  All for thee, all for thee.

4 'Neath the cross I see thee bending,
  To the place of skulls ascending,
  None attending, none befriending,
    All for me, all for me;
  Now my heart, with thy life beating,
  To each cross shall give glad greeting,
  While my lips are still repeating:
    "All for thee, all for thee."

5 In thy Father's glory sharing,
  And the crown of ages wearing,
  Thou art now a home preparing,
    All for me, all for me;
  With the souls of thy befriending,
  Saved from sorrow never ending
  Shall my song be heard ascending:
    "All for thee, all for thee."

        Rev. Alfred J. Hough.

255   MARCHING ON.

1 WITH our colors waving bright in the
    blaze of gospel light
  We are marshaled on the world's great
    field;
  We are ready for the strife and the bat-
    tle-work of life,
  Ever trusting in the Lord our shield.

Chorus.

  Glory to God! we are marching, march-
    ing on,
    Marching to a home above;
  Glory to God! we are marching, march-
    ing on,
    Happy in a Saviour's love.

2 Oft the tempter we shall meet, but we
   will not fear defeat,
   Though his arrows at our ranks may
   fly;
   Through a Saviour's mighty love, more
   than conqu'rors we shall prove,
   Shouting: "Glory be to God on high!"

3 We have girded on the sword and the
   armor of the Lord,
   We have taken up the cross he bore;
   O the trophies we shall win, O the vic-
   t'ry over sin,
   When the battle and the strife are
   o'er!

4 Soon we'll reach the pearly gate, where
   the blessèd army wait,
   Soon their welcome, welcome song
   may ring;
   When we lay our armor down, and re-
   ceive a starry crown,
   Shouting: "Glory be to God, our
   King!"

Jennie Garnett.

256   The Open Arms.

1 O why are you slighting the Saviour,
   So patient, forgiving, and true?
   The arms of his mercy are open:
   He offers a welcome to you.

Chorus.

O come to the arms that are waiting,
   They long have been waiting for you;
O come to your loving Redeemer,
   So gentle, forgiving, and true.

2 Once led as a lamb to the slaughter,
　　He suffered and languished and died;
And now, in his tender compassion,
　　He shows you his hands and his side.

3 Again the dear Saviour is calling,
　　O turn ye, for why will ye die?
Your sun may go down in a moment,
　　The arrow of death may be nigh.

4 Again the dear Saviour is pleading,
　　O look to his mercy and live!
The pleasures of time are but fleeting,
　　Then trust not the promise they give.
　　　　　　　　Henrietta E. Blair.

257

BLESSED ARE THE PURE IN HEART.

1 BLESSED are the pure in heart,
　　Soul and body holy, clean;
Washed throughout in ev'ry part,
　　Saved and cleansed from ev'ry sin.

Chorus.

Bless'd are the pure in heart,
　　They shall see our heav'nly King;
Never from his side depart,
　　Safely rest beneath his wing.

2 Such shall see our God, we read;
　　We believe this precious word;
He'll supply our ev'ry need,
　　'Tis the promise of our Lord.

3 Yes, we'll see him as he is
　　When this mortal veil is rent,

In the heav'nly land of bliss,
　When our earthly life is spent.

4 Faith e'en sees him in this life,
　Walking in his glorious light;
　'Mi l-t earth's trouole, toil, and strife,
　He is with us day and night.

　　　　　　　　　L. L. Pickett.

258

STANDING ON THE PROMISES.

1 STANDING on the promises of Christ, my
　King,
　Through eternal ages let his praises
　　ring;
　"Glory in the highest!" I will shout
　　and sing,
　Standing on the promises of God.

Chorus.

Standing, standing,
Standing on the promises of God, my
　Saviour,
Standing, standing,
I'm standing on the promises of God.

2 Standing on the promises that cannot
　fail,
　When the howling storms of doubt and
　　fear assail,
　By the living Word of God I shall pre-
　　vail,
　Standing on the promises of God.

3 Standing on the promises, I now can
　see
　Perfect, present cleansing in the blood
　　for me;

Standing in the liberty where Christ makes free,
Standing on the promises of God.

4 Standing on the promises of Christ the Lord,
Bound to him eternally by love's strong cord,
Overcoming daily with the Spirit's sword,
Standing on the promises of God.

5 Standing on the promises, I cannot fall,
List'ning every moment to the Spirit's call,
Resting on my Saviour as my all in all,
Standing on the promises of God.

R. Kelso Carter.

259 OUTSIDE THE GATE.

1 POOR, starving soul, there's room for thee,
Within thy Father's home;
Why linger still? there's bread to spare:
Come in, no longer roam;
Come in; behold, thy Father calls;
His love for thee is great;
Come in, come in—he bids thee come;
Why stand outside the gate?

Chorus.

Outside the gate, outside the gate,
O soul, no longer wait;
Come in, come in, there's room for thee,
Why stand outside the gate?

2 Thy Father waits; what keeps thee
back ?
Behold his pleading face !
His circling arms would clasp thee now:
O seek his dear embrace ;
He longs to hear thee say, "Forgive;"
He mourns thy hapless state ;
Come in, come in—he bids thee come;
Why stand outside the gate?

3 O linger not, the time is short,
Its sands are ebbing fast;
This hour is thine, improve it well—
This hour, perhaps thy last;
Come in, while yet thy Father pleads,
Slight not his love so great;
Come in, come in—he bids thee come;
Why stand outside the gate?
Henrietta E. Blair.

260 Let Me in the Life-boat.

1 CHEER up, weary sailor; your ship is
adrift,
You've lost all your bearings; your eyes
upward lift;
The shadows are breaking, and light
through the rift
Shows Jesus, swiftly coming with the
life-boat.

Chorus.

Let me in the life-boat! let me in the
life-boat!
See the storm it grandly braves !
Let me in the life-boat! let me in the
life-boat!
Jesus, bear me safely o'er the waves.

2 The seas dark and heavy sweep over
the deck,
   Your efforts no longer destruction can
check,
   Your vessel is sinking, abandon the
wreck!
     Let Jesus take and save you in the
life-boat.

3 The good gospel life-boat, eternally
planned,
   Was built by the Saviour and launched
by his hand.
   Such wonderful love we can ne'er un-
derstand,
     The love that seeks and saves us in
the life-boat.

4 And now, Christian sailor, you're truly
afloat,
   And heartily singing salvation's glad
note,
   Reach out hands of mercy, help souls to
the boat,
     And keep on getting others in the
life-boat.

5 O happy the course that no billows can
thwart,
   And whether the voyage shall be
lengthy or short,
   Our Captain will bring us to heaven's
bright port;
     All praise to him who saved us in the
life-boat.

6 Our friends over yonder, on glory's
   bright shore,
Are sending out signals, and call o'er
   and e'er,
Step into the life-boat, be saved evermore,
   O come and trust to Jesus in the life-
   boat.

7 How grandly the life-boat is riding the
   waves,
The shock of the tempest it fearlessly
   braves,
Who trust it entirely will find **that it**
   saves,
   For Christ is saving sinners in the
   life-boat.

8 When into the haven we joyously ride,
The lights of the city will brighten the
   tide,
We'll answer the shouts of the saints
   glorified,
All glory be to Jesus for his life-boat.
                                    L. H. Edmunds.

261 Will the Waters Be Chilly?

1 Show pity, Lord, O Lord, forgive;
   Prepare me, Lord, to die,
Let a repenting rebel live;
   Prepare me, Lord, to die.

Chorus.

Will the waters be chilly?
Will the waters be chilly?
   When I am called to die?

259

2 Are not thy mercies large and free?
   Prepare me, Lord, to die;
May not a sinner trust in thee?
   Prepare me, Lord, to die.

3 My sins are great, but don't surpass,
   Prepare me, Lord, to die;
The power and glory of thy grace,
   Prepare me, Lord, to die.

4 Great God, thy nature hath no bound,
   Prepare me, Lord, to die;
So let thy pard'ning love be found,
   Prepare me, Lord, to die.

5 O wash my soul from ev'ry sin,
   Prepare me, Lord, to die;
And make my guilty conscience clean,
   Prepare me, Lord, to die.

6 Here on my heart the burden lies,
   Prepare me, Lord, to die;
And past offenses pain my eyes,
   Prepare me, Lord, to die.
                              Isaac Watts.

262   Blessed Jesus.

1 Now the solemn shadows darken,
   And the daylight slowly dies,
Holy Saviour, thou wilt hearken
   When thy children's prayers arise,

Refrain.

Blessèd Jesus, blessèd Jesus,
   Look on us with loving eyes;
Blessèd Jesus, blessèd Jesus,
   Look on us with loving eyes.

2 Some are tried with doubts and dan-
    gers,
  Some have found their hearts grow
    cold,
  Some are aliens now and strangers
    To the faith they loved of old.

Refrain.

Blessèd Jesus, blessèd Jesus,
  Bring them back into the fold;
Blessèd Jesus, blessèd Jesus,
  Bring them back into the fold.

3 Some in conflict sore have striven,
    With temptation fierce and strong;
  Lord, to them let strength be given,
    If the battle should be long

Refrain.

Blessèd Jesus, blessèd Jesus,
  Change their mourning into song;
Blessèd Jesus, blessèd Jesus,
  Change their mourning into song.

4 By thy passion in the garden,
    By thine anguish on the tree,
  By that precious gift of pardon
    Won for us alone by thee.

Refrain.

Blessèd Jesus, blessèd Jesus,
  Set the sin-bound captives free;
Blessèd Jesus, Blessèd Jesus,
  Set the sin-bound captives free.

5 When our earthly day is closing,
    And the night grows still and deep,

Let us, in thine arms reposing,
  Feel thy power to save and keep.

Refrain.

Blessèd Jesus, blessèd Jesus,
  Give thine own beloved sleep;
Blessèd Jesus, blessèd Jesus,
  Give thine own beloved sleep.

John R. Sweney.

263   I'M NOT ALONE.

1 WHEN darkening shadow round me
    falls,
  And light and hope seem gone,
There is one thought my heart upholds:
  It is, I'm not alone.

Refrain.

No, never alone,
  Can Jesus' followers be;
He's ever near, why should we fear,
  Our guide and hope is he.

2 His eye can pierce the darkest cloud,
  His arm all danger stay;
He waits for neither look nor word,
  Our troubles to allay.

3 When sorrows come with crushing blow
  O'er my defenseless head;
I tremble not; for well I know
  Who by my side doth tread.

4 So cheerfully I travel on
  Through life's dark, thorny way;
I'll fear no ill, I'm not alone
  While Jesus is my stay.

Mary B. Peck.

264 Mercy is Boundless and Free.

1 Thanks be to Jesus, his mercy is free,
   Mercy is free, mercy is free;
Sinner, that mercy is flowing for thee,
   Mercy is boundless and free.

If thou art willing on him to believe,
   Mercy is free, mercy is free;
Life everlasting thy soul may receive,
   Mercy is boundless and free.

Refrain.

Jesus the Saviour is looking for thee,
   Looking for thee, looking for thee;
Lovingly, tenderly calling for thee,
   Calling and looking for thee.

2 Why on the mountains of sin wilt thou
      roam?
   Mercy is free, mercy is free;
Gently the Spirit is calling, "Come
      home,"
   Mercy is boundless and free.
Thou art in darkness, O come to the light,
   Mercy is free, mercy is free;
Jesus is waiting, he'll save you to-night,
   Mercy is boundless and free.

3 Think of his goodness, his patience and
      love,
   Mercy is free, mercy is free;
Pleading thy cause with his Father
      above,
   Mercy is boundless and free.

Come and repenting, O give him thy
heart,
Mercy is free, mercy is free;
Grieve him no longer, but come as thou
art,
Mercy is boundless and free.

4 Yes, there is pardon for all who believe,
Mercy is free, mercy is free;
Come and this moment a blessing re-
ceive,
Mercy is boundless and free.
Jesus is waiting, O hear him proclaim,
Mercy is free, mercy is free;
Cling to his mercy, believe on his name,
Mercy is boundless and free.

265 Our Cause Is Marching On.

1 WE'VE joined the glorious sisterhood,
two hundred thousand strong,
With heart and hand united for the
overthrow of wrong;
With purpose firm and courage high
our phalanx moves along,
Our cause is marching on.

Chorus.

Glory, hallelujah!
Sing, glory hallelujah!
Sing, glory hallelujah!
Our cause is marching on.

2 We've heard the cry of childhood, and
the prayer of women, too;
We've seen the fall of manhood, and
what alcohol will do;

We've consecrated heart and hand to
  push this campaign through,
Our cause is marching on.

3 With Jesus for our Captain, no ill can
  us betide;
In the secret of his power we assuredly
  confide;
Anchored to the Rock of Ages, securely
  we abide;
Our cause is marching on.

4 With his light upon our pathway, and
  his grace within our hearts,
Fearing naught that man can do to us,
  nor dreading Satan's dart,
Leaning hard on our Belovèd, from
  whose strength we ne'er shall part,
Our cause is marching on.

5 A better day is dawning, the hour is
  drawing near,
King Alcohol shall be dethroned, with
  all that he holds dear,
And peace and plenty crown our land,
  spreading ev'rywhere,
Our cause is marching on.
                    Mrs. Fanny H. Carr.

266

WHAT WILL THE FIRST GREETING BE?

1 I HAVE heard of a land, of a beautiful
  land,
That is over the dark rolling sea,
And I know there are joys that are
  waiting me there,
But what will the first greeting be?

Chorus.

There'll be music, there'll be singing,
And throughout all heaven ringing
    There'll be shouts of hallelujah o'er
    and o'er;
But I know the first to meet me,
And with welcome smile to greet me,
    Will be Jesus, when I reach the gold-
    en shore.

2 O I know that my Saviour has gone to
    prepare,
    In his kingdom, a mansion for me,
And I know there's a crown and a robe
    and a song,
    But what will the first greeting be?

3 Many loved ones have gone to that
    bright, happy land,
    But their faces again I shall see;
And we'll clasp their glad hands on that
    beautiful strand,
    But what will the first greeting be?

4 When I pass through the vale of the
    shadow of death
    To that land where the weary are free,
I shall join in the song of the purified
    throng,
    But what will the first greeting be?
                                    P. H. Dingman.

267 HEAR AND ANSWER PRAYER.

1 I AM praying, blessèd Saviour,
    To be more and more like thee;
  I am praying that thy Spirit
    Like a dove may rest on me.

Chorus.

Thou who knowest all my weakness,
　Thou who knowest all my care,
While I plead each precious promise,
　Hear, O hear, and answer prayer.

2 I am praying, blessèd Saviour,
　　For a faith so clear and bright,
That its eye will see thy glory
　　Through the deepest, darkest night.

3 I am praying to be humbled
　　By the pow'r of grace divine,
To be clothed upon with meekness,
　　And to have no will but thine.

4 I am praying, blessèd Saviour,
　　And my constant prayer shall be
For a perfect consecration,
　　That shall make me more like thee.
　　　　　　Fanny J. Crosby.

268　　Just Ahead.

1 'Mid the toil and the battle, I think of
　my home,
Where the sound of life's conflicts can
　never more come;
Where the angel of peace spreads his
　wings o'er the scene,
And eternity's sea is all calm and serene.

Chorus.

Just ahead, just ahead, I see the pearly
　gates unfold,
And hear the harps of shining gold,

Where blood - bought saints the new
· song sing
To him who redeemed us, our blessèd
King.

2 By the bank of life's river our loved we
shall greet,
With them shall rejoice in a rapture
complete;
Shall join in the song that the glorified
sing,
While the arches of heaven shall tremble and ring.

3 There cherubs effulgent and seraphs
that blaze
May join in our anthem of rapturous
praise;
And the Son that was given the world
to redeem,
Shall be of our joying and praising the
theme.

4 As year after year shall fly swiftly away,
And yet but begun is eternity's day;
While springs of new pleasure delight-
eth the soul,
While onward, yet onward, the ages
shall roll.

5 Prepare, then, ye faithful, to enter your
land,
The mansion prepared by the Saviour's
own hand.
'Tis ready, now waiting, so beauteous
·and fair,
Then bind on your sandals, we soon
shall be there.

Edgar Page. Cho. by *H. L. Gilmour.*

269   On the Way.

1 O BLESS the Lord, what joy is mine!
   What perfect peace through grace di-
      vine!
   And now to realms of endless day,
   O bless the Lord, I'm on the way.

Chorus.

I'm on the way, I'm on the way,
In vain the world would bid me stay;
A crown to wear in endless day,
O bless the Lord, I'm on the way.

2 O bless the Lord, he dwells with me,
   The voice I hear, the hand I see;
   Renew my strength from day to day,
   While home to him I'm on the way.

3 O bless the Lord for what I know
   Of heav'nly bliss while here below;
   My trusting heart through faith can say,
   To mansions bright I'm on the way.

4 O bless the Lord, 'twill not be long
   Till I shall join the holy throng,
   And shout and sing through endless day,
   Where ev'ry tear is wiped away.
                           Lizzie Edwards.

270   I Am Safe.

1 OFT when tossed on ocean's foam,
   As I voyage to my home,
      And no ray of light about I see;
   With my bark the sport of wave,
   When no human arm can save,
      Unto Jesus in my fear I flee.

Chorus.

What though mountain billows threaten,
   and the clouds above me roll!
I am safe if Jesus only of my bark shall
   take control;
I can brave the wildest tempest if his
   glory fills my soul,
   I can sing amid its raging and rejoice.

2 He can cheer the darkest night,
  He can flood the soul with light,
   He can scatter all our fears away;
  He will hear the honest cry,   •
  And all needed grace supply,
   Sending answers even while we pray.

3 Knowing this, I courage take;
  He will never me forsake,
   But my trials help me bear instead;
  They are only for my good,
  And when all is understood
   I shall thank him for the way he led.
               F. A. Blackmer.

271

A HEART FROM SIN SET FREE.

1 O FOR a heart to praise my God,
  A heart from sin set free;
  A heart that always feels thy blood,
  So freely spilt for me.

Chorus.

A heart from sin set free,
  'Tis of thy grace divine:
O Lord, I know 'tis all for me,
  The glory shall be thine

2 A heart resigned, submissive, meek,
 My great Redeemer's throne;
Where only Christ is heard to speak,
 Where Jesus reigns alone.

3 O for a lowly, contrite heart,
 Believing, true, and clean,
Which neither life nor death can part
 From him that dwells within!

4 A heart in ev'ry thought renewed,
 And full of love divine:
Perfect and right and pure and good,
 A copy, Lord, of thine.

5 Thy nature, gracious Lord, impart;
 Come quickly from above;
Write thy new name upon my heart,
 Thy new, best name of love.
      Charles Wesley.

272 Happy Tidings.

1 Tidings, happy tidings,
 Hark! hark! the sound!
Hear the joyful echo
 Through the world resound;
Christ the Lord proclaims them,
 Hear and heed the call:
" Come, ye starving ones that perish,
 Room, room for all."

   Refrain.

Whosoever asketh,
 Jesus will receive;
Whosoever thirsteth,
 Jesus will relieve;

See the living waters,
  Flowing full and free;
O the blessèd whosoever!
  That means me.

2 Tidings, happy tidings,
    Hark! hark! they say,
  Do not slight the warning,
    Come, O come to-day;
  Christ, our loving Saviour,
    Still repeats the call:
  "Come, ye weary, heavy laden,"
    Room, room for all."

3 Tidings, happy tidings,
    Hark! hark! again!
  Rushing o'er the mountain,
    Sweeping o'er the plain;
  Onward goes the message,
    'Tis the Saviour's call:
  "Come, for ev'ry thing is ready,
    Room, room for all."

Lizzie Edwards.

273 Bringing in the Sheaves.

1 Sowing in the morning, sowing seeds of
    kindness,
  Sowing in the noontide, and the dewy
    eves;
  Waiting for the harvest, and the time of
    reaping,
  We shall come rejoicing, bringing in
    the sheaves.

Chorus.

Bringing in the sheaves, bringing in the
    sheaves,
  We shall come rejoicing, bringing in
    the sheaves;
Bringing in the sheaves, bringing in the
    sheaves,
  We shall come rejoicing, bringing in
    the sheaves.

2 Sowing in the sunshine, sowing in the
    shadows,
  Fearing neither clouds nor winter's
    chilly breeze;
By and by the harvest, and the labor
    ended,
  We shall come rejoicing, bringing in
    the sheaves.

3 Go, then, ever weeping, sowing for the
    Master,
Though the loss sustained our spirit often
    grieves;
  When our weeping's over, he will bid
    us welcome,
We shall come rejoicing, bringing in
    the sheaves.
        Words from " Songs of Glory."

274   Are You Ready?

1 Should the summons, quickly flying,
  On the slumb'ring nations fall,
Lo! the heav'nly Bridegroom cometh,
  Would the sound your souls appall?

18   273

Chorus.

Are you ready? are you ready,
　Should you hear the midnight call?
Are you ready? are you ready,
　Should you hear the midnight call?

2 What if now the startling mandate
　Should the sleeping virgins hear?
Are your lamps all trimmed and burn-
　ing,
　Should the Bridegroom now appear?

Chorus.

Are you ready? are you ready,
　Now to see your Lord appear?
Are you ready? are you ready,
　Now to see your Lord appear?

3 Is there oil in all your vessels?
　Are your garments pure and white?
Are they washed in the cleansing fount-
　ain,
　Fit to stand in Jesus' sight?

Chorus.

Are you ready? are you ready,
　Are your lamps all clear and bright?
Are you ready? are you ready,
　Are your lamps all clear and bright?

4 Rise, ye virgins; sleep no longer,
　Lest the call your soul surprise!
Lest ye fail to meet the Bridegroom,
　When he cometh from the skies.

Chorus.

O be ready! O be ready,
    When he cometh from the skies;
O be ready! O be ready,
    Hrsten, from your slumbers rise!
                   Mary D. James.

275   JESUS SAVES.

1 WE have heard a joyful sound,
    Jesus saves, Jesus saves;
Spread the gladness all around,
    Jesus saves, Jesus saves;
Bear the news to ev'ry land,
    Climb the steeps and cross the waves,
Onward, 'tis our Lord's command,
    Jesus saves, Jesus saves.

2 Waft it on the rolling tide,
    Jesus saves, Jesus saves;
Tell to sinners far and wide,
    Jesus saves, Jesus saves;
Sing, ye islands of the sea;
    Echo back, ye ocean caves;
Earth shall keep her jubilee,
    Jesus saves, Jesus saves.

3 Sing above the battle strife,
    Jesus saves, Jesus saves;
By his death and endless life,
    Jesus saves, Jesus saves;
Sing it softly through the gloom,
    When the heart of mercy craves,
Sing in triumph o'er the tomb,
    Jesus saves, Jesus saves.

4 Give the winds a mighty voice,
   Jesus saves, Jesus saves;
Let the nations now rejoice,
   Jesus saves, Jesus saves;
Shout salvation full and free,
   Highest hills and deepest caves,
This our song of victory,
   Jesus saves, Jesus saves.
                                    Priscilla J. Owens.

276   SINNER, TURN.

1 SINNERS, turn; why will ye die;
God your Maker asks you why;
God, who did your being give,
Made you with himself to live;
He the fatal cause demands:
Asks the work of his own hands,
Why, ye thankless creatures, why
Will ye cross his love and die?

Chorus.

Sinner, turn; O sinner, turn;
   Turn, O turn, why will you die?
Sinner, turn; O sinner, turn;
   Turn, O turn, why will you die?

2 Sinners, turn; why will you die?
   God your Saviour asks ye why;
He who did your souls retrieve,
   Died himself that ye might live
Will ye let him die in vain?
   Crucify your Lord again?
Why, ye ransomed sinners, why
   Will ye slight his grace and die?
                            276

3 Sinners, turn; why will ye die?
  God the Spirit asks you why;
He who all your lives hath strove,
  Wooed you to embrace his love.
Will ye not his grace receive?
  Will ye still refuse to live?
Why, ye long sought sinners, why
  Will ye grieve your God and die?
Charles Wesley.

277   Welcome Home.

1 O when shall I sweep through the gates?
  The scenes of mortality o'er,
What then for my spirit awaits?
  Will they sing on the beautiful shore?

Refrain.

Welcome home! welcome home!
  A welcome in glory for me;
Welcome home! welcome home!
  A welcome for me.

2 When from Calvary's mount I rise,
  And pass through the portals above,
Will shouts, "Welcome home to the skies!"
  Resound through the regions of love?

3 Yes; loved ones who knew me below,
  Who learned the new song with me here,
In chorus will hail me, I know,
  And welcome me home with good cheer.

4 The beautiful gates will unfold,
  The home of the blood-washed I'll
    see;
  The city of saints I'll behold,
  For O there's a welcome for me

5 A sinner made whiter than snow,
  I'll join in the mighty acclaim,
  And shout through the gates as I go:
  "Salvation to God and the Lamb!"
  Mrs. Phœbe Palmer.

278 STEPPING IN THE LIGHT.

1 TRYING to walk in the steps of the Sav-
    iour,
  Trying to follow our Saviour and
    King;
  Shaping our lives by his blessèd example,
  Happy, how happy, the songs that we
    bring!

Chorus.

How beautiful to walk in the steps of
  the Saviour,
  Stepping in the light, stepping in the
    light!
How beautiful to walk in the steps of
  the Saviour,
  Led in paths of light!

2 Pressing more closely to him who is
    leading,
  When we are tempted to turn from
    the way;
  Trusting the arm that is strong to de-
    fend us,
  Happy, how happy our praises each
    day.

3 Walking in footsteps of gentle forbear-
ance,
  Footsteps of faithfulness, mercy, and
  love,
  Looking to him for the grace freely
  promised,
  Happy, how happy our journey above!

4 Trying to walk in the steps of the Sav-
iour,
  Upward, still upward, we'll follow our
  Guide;
  When we shall see him, "the King in
  his beauty,"
  Happy, how happy our place at his
  side!

L. H. Edmunds.

279
TELL ME THE STORY OF JESUS.

1 TELL me the story of Jesus,
  Write on my heart ev'ry word;
Tell me the story most precious,
  Sweetest that ever was heard;
Tell how the angels, in chorus,
  Sang as they welcomed his birth:
"Glory to God in the highest!
  Peace and good tidings to earth."

Chorus.

Tell me the story of Jesus,
  Write on my heart ev'ry word;
Tell me the story most precious,
  Sweetest that ever was heard.

2 Fasting, alone in the desert,
   Tell of the days that he passed:
How for our sins he was tempted,
   Yet was triumphant at last,
Tell of the years of his labor,
   Tell of the sorrow he bore;
He was despised and afflicted,
   Homeless, rejected, and poor.

3 Tell of the cross where they nailed him,
   Writhing in anguish and pain;
Tell of the grave where they laid him,
   Tell how he liveth again;
Love, in that story so tender,
   Clearer than ever I see;
Stay, let me weep while you whisper,
   Love paid the ransom for me.

Fanny J. Crosby.

280   DRAW ME TO THEE.

1 OUT on the midnight deep,
   Hear thou my cry;
Come to my rescue, Lord,
   Save or I die.
Let not the stormy waves
   Break over me;
Reach out thy loving arm,
   Draw me to thee.

Chorus.

Draw me to thee, Saviour,
   Draw me to thee;
Reach out thy loving arm,
   Draw me to thee.

2 Hope of the desolate,
  Light of the soul,
Now of my lonely bark
  Take thou control;
Yonder the Ark of Grace
  Dimly I see;
Reach out thy loving arm,
  Draw me to thee.

3 Lord, at the open door,
  Let me come in;
Heal thou my broken heart,
  Weary of sin;
Close to thy bleeding side
  Still would I be,
Reach out thy loving arm,
  Draw me to thee.

Fanny J. Crosby.

281 HARVEST TIME.

1 THE seed I have scattered in spring-
    time with weeping,
  And watered with tears and with
    dews from on high;
Another may shout when the harvesters,
    reaping,
  Shall gather my grain in the "sweet
  by and by."

Chorus.

Over and over, yes, deeper and deeper
  My heart is pierced through with life's
    sorrowing cry,
But the tears of the sower and songs of
    the reaper
  Shall mingle together in joy by and
  by.

By and by, by and by,
By and by, by and by;
Yes, the tears of the sower, and songs
    of the reaper
    Shall mingle together in joy by and
    by.

2 Another may reap what in spring-time
    I've planted,
    Another rejoice in the fruit of my
    pain,
    Not knowing my tears when in summer
    I fainted
    While toiling, sad-hearted, in sun-
    shine and rain.

3 The thorns will have choked, and the
    summer sun blasted
    The most of the seed which in spring-
    time I've sown;
    But the Lord, who has watched while
    my weary toil lasted,
    Will give me a harvest for what I have
    done.

Rev. W. A. Spencer.

282   Tell It Out.

1 Tell it out among the nations that the
    Lord is King;
    Tell it out! tell it out!
    Tell it out among the heathen, bid them
    shout and sing;
    Tell it out! tell it out!
    Tell it out with adoration that he shall
    increase,

That the mighty King of Glory is the
    King of Peace;
    Tell it out! tell it out!
Tell it out with jubilation, let the songs
    ne'er cease;
    Tell it out! tell it out!

2 Tell it out among the nations that the
    Saviour reigns;
    Tell it out! tell it out!
Tell it out among the heathen, bid them
    break their chains;
    Tell it out! tell it out!
Tell it out among the weeping ones that
    Jesus lives;
Tell it out among the weary ones what
    rest he gives;
    Tell it out! tell it out!
Tell it out among the sinners that he
    came to save;
    Tell it out! tell it out!

3 Tell it out among the nations, Jesus
    reigns above;
    Tell it out! tell it out!
Tell it out among the heathen that his
    reign is love;
    Tell it out! tell it out!
Tell it out among the highways and the
    lawns at home;
Let it ring across the mountains and the
    ocean's foam;
    Tell it out! tell it out!
Like the voice of many waters let **our**
    glad shout be:
    "Tell it out! tell it out!"
                Frances Ridley Havergal.

283 What Must I Do To Be Saved?

1 O what must I do to be saved
　　From the guilt and dominion of sin?
　From its fetters and chains,
　From its manifold stains,
　　Who will free me? who will cleanse
　　me within?

Chorus.

　O what must I do? what must I do?
　O what must I do to be saved?

2 O what must I do to be saved?
　　For the moments are fast gliding by;
　For eternity's near,
　The great judgment I fear,
　　Soon the summons will come from on
　　high.

3 O what must I do to be saved?
　　Let me turn unto God's blessèd book;
　For it bids me "believe,"
　And salvation receive,
　　While on Jesus, Redeemer, I look.

4 O this I must do to be saved:
　　I will come to the Saviour this hour;
　I will come to his cross,
　And all else count but dross,
　　I will yield to his life-giving power.
　　　　　　　　　　E. E. Hewitt.

284　Jesus, Lover of My Soul.

1 Jesus, lover of my soul,
　　Let me to thy bosom fly,
　While the nearer waters roll,
　　While the tempest still is high.

Hide me, O my Saviour, hide,
  Till the storm of life is past;
Safe into the haven guide,
  O receive my soul at last,
  O receive my soul at last.

2 Other refuge have I none,
    Hangs my helpless soul on thee;
  Leave, O leave me not alone,
    Still support and comfort me.
  All my trust on thee is staid,
    All my help from thee I bring;
  Cover my defenseless head
    With the shadow of thy wing,
    With the shadow of thy wing.

3 Thou, O Christ, art all I want;
    More than all in thee I find;
  Raise the fallen, cheer the faint,
    Heal the sick, and lead the blind.
  Just and holy is thy name,
    I am all unrighteousness,
  False and full of sin I am,
    Thou art full of truth and grace,
    Thou art full of truth and grace.

4 Plenteous grace with thee is found,
    Grace to cover all my sin;
  Let the healing streams abound;
    Make and keep me pure within.
  Thou of life the fountain art,
    Freely let me take of thee;
  Spring thou up within my heart,
    Rise to all eternity,
    Rise to all eternity.
                    Charles Wesley.

285 MY FATHERLAND.

1 THERE is a place where the angels dwell,
A pure and a peaceful abode ;
The joys of that place no tongue can tell,
But there is the palace of God.

Chorus.

I'm bound for home, for my fatherland,
The house and the city above;
And soon shall I join the ransomed band,
And dwell in that city of love.

2 There is a place where they never die,
Where beauty and youth never fade;
Where never is heard the mournful cry:
"My friend, my beloved, is dead."

3 There is a place where my friends have
gone,
Who suffered and worshiped with me,
Exalted with Christ, high on his throne,
The King in his beauty they see.

4 There is a place where I hope to live,
When life and its labors are o'er;
A place which the Lord to me will give,
And then I shall sorrow no more.
Rev. W. Hunter.

286 COME, YE SINNERS.

1 COME, ye sinners, poor and needy,
Weak and wounded, sick and sore;
Jesus ready stands to save you,
Full of pity, love, and power.

He is able,
He is willing, ·
He is able,
He is willing, doubt no more;
He is able,
He is willing,
He is able,
He is willing, doubt no more.

2 Now, ye needy, come and welcome;
    God's free bounty glorify;
True belief and true repentance,
    Ev'ry grace that brings you nigh.
        Without money,
        Without money,
        Without money,
Come to Jesus Christ and buy;
        Without money,
        Without money,
        Without money,
Come to Jesus Christ and buy.

3 Come, ye weary, heavy laden,
    Bruised and mangled by the fall;
If you tarry till you're better,
    You will never come at all.
        Not the righteous,
        Not the righteous,
        Not the righteous:
Sinners, Jesus came to call;
        Not the righteous,
        Not the righteous,
        Not the righteous:
· Sinners, Jesus came to call,

4 Lo! th' incarnate God, ascending,
  Pleads the merit of his blood:
Venture on him, venture freely;
  Let no other trust intrude.
            None but Jesus,
            None but Jesus,
            None but Jesus
  Can do helpless sinners good:
            None but Jesus,
            None but Jesus,
            None but Jesus
  Can do helpless sinners good.
                              Joseph Hart.

287 WHY DON'T YOU COME TO JESUS?

1 COME, ye sinners, poor and needy,
    Weak and wounded, sick and sore;
  Jesus ready stands to save you,
    Full of pity, love, and power.

Refrain.

    Why don't you come to Jesus?
      He's waiting to receive you,
    Why dont you come to Jesus and be
      saved?
    Why don't you come to Jesus?
      He's waiting to receive you,
    Why don't you come to Jesus and be
      saved?

2 Now, ye needy, come and welcome;
    God's free bounty glorify;
  True belief and true repentance,
    Ev'ry grace that brings you nigh.

288

3 Come, ye weary, heavy laden,
　　Bruised and mangled by the fall;
If you tarry till you're better,
　　You will never come at all.

4 Lo! th' incarnate God, ascending,
　　Pleads the merit of his blood;
Venture on him, venture freely,
　　Let no other trust intrude.
Joseph Hart.

288　We'll Work Till Jesus Comes.

1 O LAND of rest, for thee I sigh,
　　When will the moment come,
When I shall lay my armor by
　　And dwell in peace at home?

Chorus.

We'll work till Jesus comes,
We'll work till Jesus comes,
We'll work till Jesus comes,
　　And we'll be gathered home.

' No tranquil joys on earth I know,
　　No peaceful, shelt'ring dome;
This world's a wilderness of woe,
　　This world is not my home.

3 To Jesus Christ I fled for rest;
　　He bade me cease to roam,
And lean for succor on his breast,
　　Till he conduct me home.

4 I sought at once my Saviour's side,
　　No more my steps shall roam;
With him I'll brave death's chilling tide,
　　And reach my heav'nly home.
Mrs. Elizabeth Mills.

289 HAPPY LAND.

1 THERE is a happy land,
    Far, far away;
  Where saints in glory stand,
    Bright, bright as day.
  O how they sweetly sing,
  "Worthy is our Saviour King!"
  Loud let his praises ring,
    Praise, praise for aye.

2 Bright, in that happy land,
    Beams ev'ry eye;
  Kept by a Father's hand,
    Love cannot die.
  On, then, to glory run;
  Be a crown and kingdom won;
  And bright, above the sun,
    Reign evermore.

3 Come to that happy land,
    Come, come away;
  Why will you doubting stand?
    Why still delay?
  O we shall happy be,
  When from sin and sorrow free;
  Lord, we shall dwell with thee,
    Blest evermore.

290 JESUS SAVES ME.

1 PRECIOUS Saviour, thou hast saved me;
    Thine, and only thine I am;
  O the cleansing blood has reached me,
    Glory, glory to the Lamb!

Refrain.

Glory, glory, Jesus saves me,
　Glory, glory to the Lamb!
O the cleansing blood has reached me,
　Glory, glory to the Lamb!

2 Long my yearning heart was trying
　　To enjoy this perfect rest;
　But I gave all trying over:
　　Simply trusting; I was blest.

3 Trusting, trusting every moment;
　　Feeling now the blood applied;
　Lying at the cleansing fountain,
　　Dwelling in my Saviour's side.

4 Consecrated to thy service,
　　I will live and die to thee;
　I will witness to thy glory
　　Of salvation full and free.

5 Yes, I will stand up for Jesus;
　　He has sweetly saved my soul,
　Cleansed me from inbred corruption,
　　Sanctified and made me whole.

6 Glory to the blood that bought me,
　　Glory to its cleansing power!
　Glory to the blood that keeps me!
　　Glory, glory evermore!
　　　　　　Louise M. Rouse.

291　　I Have Sought.

1 I HAVE sought round the verdant earth
　　For unfading joy;
　I have tried ev'ry source of mirth,
　　But all, all will cloy;

Lord, bestow on me
Grace to set my spirit free;
Thine the praise shall be,
    Mine, mine the joy.

2 I have wandered in mazes dark
    Of doubt and distress;
I have had not a kindling spark,
    My spirit to bless;
Cheerless unbelief
Filled my lab'ring soul with grief;
What shall give relief?
    What shall give peace?

3 Then I turned to thy gospel, Lord,
    From folly away;
Then I trusted thy holy word
    That taught me to pray;
Here I found release,
In thy word my soul found peace,
Hope of endless bliss,
    Eternal day.

4 I will praise now my heav'nly King,
    I'll praise and adore;
All my heart's richest tribute bring,
    To thee, God of power;
And in heav'n above,
Saved by thy redeeming love,
Loud the strains shall move
    For evermore.

292   I Am Coming to the Cross.

1 I am coming to the cross,
    I am poor and weak and blind·
I am counting all but dross,
    I shall full salvation find.

Chorus.

I am trusting, Lord, in thee,
Blest Lamb of Calvary;
Humbly at thy cross I bow,
Save me, Jesus, save me now.

2 Long my heart has sighed for thee,
   Long has evil dwelt within;
Jesus sweetly speaks to me:
   " I will cleanse you from all sin."

3 Here I give my all to thee,
   Friends and time and earthly
     store;
Soul and body thine to be,
   Wholly thine for evermore.

4 In thy promises I trust,
   Now I feel the blood applied;
I am prostrate in the dust,
   I with Christ am crucified.

5 Jesus comes! he fills my soul!
   Perfected in love I am;
I am ev'ry whit made whole:
   Glory, glory to the Lamb!
       Rev. William McDonald.

293   Rest for the Weary.

1 In the Christian's home in glory
   There remains a land of rest;
There my Saviour's gone before me,
   To fulfill my soul's request.

Chorus.

There is rest for the weary,
There is rest for the weary,
There is rest for the weary,
    There is rest for you;
On the other side the river,
In the sweet fields of Eden,
Where the tree of life is blooming,
    There is rest for you.

2 Pain or sickness ne'er shall enter,
    Grief nor woe my lot shall share;
But in that celestial center,
    I a crown of life shall wear.

3 Death itself shall then be vanquished,
    And his sting shall be withdrawn:
Shout for gladness, O ye ransomed!
    Hail with joy the rising morn.

4 Sing, O sing, ye heirs of glory;
    Shout your triumph as you go;
Zion's gates will open for you,
    You shall find an entrance through.
                Rev. S. G. Harmer.

294   REVIVE US AGAIN.

1 WE praise thee, O God! for the Son of
    thy love,
For Jesus who died and is now gone
    above.

Refrain.

Hallelujah! thine the glory;
    Hallelujah! Amen!
Hallelujah! thine the glory;
    Revive us again.

2 We praise thee, O God! for thy Spirit of
    light,
  Who has shown us our Saviour and
    scattered our night.

3 All glory and praise to the Lamb that
    was slain,
  Who has borne all our sins, and has
    cleansed ev'ry stain.

4 All glory and praise to the God of all
    grace,
  Who has bought us and sought us and
    guided our ways.

5 Revive us again; fill each heart with
    thy love;
  May each soul be rekindled with fire
    from above!
                    William P. Macky.

295   ALL FOR JESUS.

1 ALL for Jesus! all for Jesus!
    All my being's ransomed powers;
  All my thoughts and words and doings,
    All my days and all my hours.
      All for Jesus! all for Jesus!
    All my days and all my hours.

2 Let my hands perform his bidding,
    Let my feet run in his ways,
  Let my eyes see Jesus only.
    Let my lips speak forth his praise.
      All for Jesus! all for Jesus!
    Let my lips speak forth his praise.

3 Since my eyes were fixed on Jesus,
  I've lost sight of all besides;
So enchained my spirit's vision
  Looking at the Crucified.
    All for Jesus! all for Jesus!
  Looking at the Crucified.

4 O what wonder! how amazing!
  Jesus, glorious King of kings;
Deigns to call me his beloved,
  Let's me rest beneath his wings.
    All for Jesus! all for Jesus!
  Resting now beneath his wings.
        Mary D. James.

296 Come, Ye Disconsolate.

1 Come, ye disconsolate, where'er ye languish;
  Come to the mercy-seat, fervently kneel;
  Here bring your wounded hearts, here tell your anguish;
  Earth has no sorrow that heav'n cannot heal.

2 Joy of the desolate, light of the straying,
  Hope of the penitent, fadeless and pure.
  Here speaks the Comforter, tenderly saying:
  "Earth hath no sorrow that heav'n cannot cure."

3 Here see the bread of life; see waters
  flowing
   Forth from the throne of God, pure
   from above.
  Come to the feast of love; come, ever
  knowing
   Earth has no sorrow but heav'n can
   remove.

Thomas Moore (alt.)
And Thomas Hastings.

297　　　At the Fountain.

1 Of him who did salvation bring,
   I'm at the fountain drinking;
  I could forever think and sing,
   I'm on my journey home.

Chorus.

   Glory to God.
  I'm at the fountain drinking:
   Glory to God,
  I'm on my journey home.

2 Ask but his grace and lo! 'tis given,
   I'm at the fountain drinking;
  Ask and he turns your hell to heaven,
   I'm on my journey home.

3 Though sin and sorrow wound my soul,
   I'm at the fountain drinking;
  Jesus, thy balm will make me whole,
   I'm on my journey home.

4 Where'er I am, where'er I move,
   I'm at the fountain drinking;
  I meet the object of my love,
   I'm on my journey home.

5 Insatiate to this spring I fly,
   I'm at the fountain drinking;
I drink, and yet I'm ever dry,
   I'm on my journey home.

Chorus.

   Glory to God,
I'm at the fountain drinking;
   Glory to God,
My soul is satisfied.

298   HAPPY DAY.

1 O HAPPY day that fixed my choice
   On thee my Saviour and my God!
Well may this glowing heart rejoice,
   And tell its raptures all abroad.

Chorus.

   Happy day, happy day,
When Jesus washed my sins away!
He taught me how to watch and pray,
   And live rejoicing ev'ry day;
Happy day, happy day,
   When Jesus washed my sins away.

2 O happy bond that seals my vows
   To him who merits all my love!
Let cheerful anthems fill his house,
   While to that sacred shrine I move.

3 'Tis done, the great transaction's done!
   I am my Lord's and he is mine:
He drew me and I followed on,
   Charmed to confess that voice divine.

4 Now rest, my long-divided heart;
    Fixed on this blissful center, rest;
Nor ever from thy Lord depart;
    With him of ev'ry good possessed.

5 High heav'n that heard the solemn vow,
    That vow renewed shall daily hear,
Till in life's latest hour I bow,
    And bless in death a bond so dear.
                    P. Doddridge.

299   He Came to Save Me.

1 WHEN Jesus laid his crown aside,
    He came to save me;
When on the cross he bled and died,
    He came to save me.

Refrain.

    I'm so glad, I'm so glad,
    I'm so glad that Jesus came;
    And grace is free,
    He came to save me.

2 In my poor heart he deigns to dwell
    He came to save me.
O praise his name, I know it well,
    He came to save me.

3 With gentle hand he leads me still,
    He came to save me;
And trusting him I fear no ill,
    He came to save me.

4 To him my faith with rapture clings,
    He came to save me;
To him my heart looks up and sings,
    He came to save me.
                  H. E. Blair.

300 O 'Tis Glory in My Soul.

1 To thy cross, dear Christ, I'm clinging,
　　All my refuge and my plea;
　Matchless is thy loving-kindness,
　　Else it had not stooped to me.

Chorus.

　O 'tis glory! O 'tis glory!
　　O 'tis glory in my soul,
　For I've touched the hem of his gar-
　　ment,
　　And his pow'r doth make me whole.

2 Long my heart hath heard thee calling,
　　But I thrust aside thy grace;
　Yet, O boundless condescension,
　　Love is shining from thy face.

3 Love eternal, light eternal,
　　Close me safely, sweetly in;
　Saviour, let thy balm of healing,
　　Ever keep me free from sin.
　　　　　　　　　　Flora L. Best.

301 Come, Thou Fount.

I Come thou Fount of ev'ry blessing,
　　Tune my heart to sing thy grace,
　Streams of mercy, never ceasing,
　　Call for songs of loudest praise.
　Teach me some melodious sonnet,
　　Sung by flaming tongues above;
　Praise the mount—I'm fixed upon it,
　　Mount of thy redeeming love.

2 Here I raise mine Ebenezer,
    Hither by thy help I'm come;
And I hope by thy good pleasure,
    Safely to arrive at home.
Jesus sought me when a stranger,
    Wand'ring from the fold of God;
He, to rescue me from danger,
    Interposed his precious blood.

3 O to grace how great a debtor
    Daily I'm constrained to be!
Let thy goodness like a fetter,
    Bind my wand'ring heart to thee.
Prone to wander, Lord, I feel it,
    Prone to leave the God I love;
Here's my heart, O take and seal it;
    Seal it for thy courts above.
                    Robert Robinson.

302   COME TO JESUS.

1 COME to Jesus,
    Come to Jesus,
    Come to Jesus just now,
    Just now come to Jesus,
    Come to Jesus just now.

2 He will save you,
    He will save you,
    He will save you just now,
    Just now he will save you,
    He will save you just now.

3 He is able,
    He is able,
    He is able just now,
    Just now he is able,
    He is able just now.

4 He is willing,
 He is willing,
 He is willing just now,
 Just now he is willing,
 He is willing just now.

5 He is waiting,
 He is waiting,
 He is waiting just now,
 Just now he is waiting,
 He is waiting just now.

6 O believe him,
 O believe him,
 O believe him just now,
 Just now O believe him,
 O believe him just now.

7 He will bless you,
 He will bless you,
 He will bless you just now,
 Just now he will bless you,
 He will bless you just now.

303   Glory to His Name.

1 Down at the cross where my Saviour
  died,
 Down where for cleansing from sin I
  cried;
 There to my heart was the blood applied;
 Glory to his name.

Chorus.

Glory to his name,
Glory to his name,

There to my heart was the blood applied;
  Glory to his name.

2 I am so wondrously saved from sin,
Jesus so sweetly abides within;
There at the cross where he took me in;
  Glory to his name.

3 O precious fountain that saves from sin!
I am so glad I have entered in;
There Jesus saves me and keeps me
 clean;
  Glory to his name.

4 Come to this fountain so rich and sweet;
Cast thy poor soul at the Saviour's feet;
Plunge in to-day and be made complete;
  Glory to his name.
                         Rev. E. A. Hoffman.

304

FROM GREENLAND'S ICY MOUNTAINS.

1 FROM Greenland's icy mountains,
   From India's coral strand;
  Where Afric's sunny fountains
   Roll down their golden sand;
  From many an ancient river,
   From many a balmy plain,
  They call us to deliver
   Their land from error's chain.

2 What though the spicy breezes
   Blow soft o'er Ceylon's Isle;
  Though ev'ry prospect pleases,
   And only man is vile:

In vain with lavish kindness
　The gifts of God are strewn;
The heathen, in his blindness,
　Bows down to wood and stone.

3 Shall we, whose souls are lighted
　With wisdom from on high,
Shall we to men benighted
　The lamp of life deny?
Salvation! O salvation!
　The joyful sound proclaim,
Till earth's remotest nation
　Has learned Messiah's name.

4 Waft, waft, ye winds, his story,
　And you, ye waters, roll,
Till, like a sea of glory,
　It spreads from pole to pole;
Till o'er our ransomed nature
　The Lamb for sinners slain,
Redeemer, King, Creator,
　In bliss returns to reign.
Reginald Heber.

305

NEARER, MY GOD, TO THEE.

1 NEARER, my God, to thee!
　Nearer to thee,
E'en though it be a cross
　That raiseth me;
Still all my song shall be,
Nearer, my God, to thee,
Nearer, my God, to thee,
　Nearer to thee.

2 Though like the wanderer,
    The sun gone down,
Darkness be over me,
    My rest a stone,
Yet in my dreams I'd be
Nearer, my God, to thee,
Nearer, my God, to thee,
    Nearer to thee.

3 There let the way appear,
    Steps unto heav'n;
All that thou sendest me,
    In mercy giv'n;
Angels to beckon me
Nearer, my God, to thee,
Nearer, my God, to thee,
    Nearer to thee.

4 Then, with my waking thoughts
    Bright with thy praise,
Out of my stony griefs
    Bethel I'll raise;
So by my woes to be
Nearer, my God, to thee,
Nearer, my God, to thee,
    Nearer to thee.

5 Or if, on joyful wing
    Cleaving the sky,
Sun, moon, and stars forgot,
    Upward I fly;
Still all my song shall be
Nearer, my God, to thee,
Nearer, my God, to thee,
    Nearer to thee.

20   305

306 O Tell Me No More.

1 O tell me no more
Of this world's vain store,
    The time for such trifles
With me now is o'er;
A country I've found
Where true joys abound;
    To dwell I'm determined
On that happy ground.

Chorus.

I'll drink when I'm dry,
I'll drink a supply,
I'll drink from the fountain
That never runs dry.

2 The souls that believe
In paradise live,
    And me in that number
Will Jesus receive;
My soul, don't delay;
He calls thee away;
    Rise, follow thy Saviour,
And bless the glad day.

3 No mortal doth know
What he can bestow,
    What light, strength, and **comfort--**
Go after him, go!
Lo, onward I move
To a city above,
    None guesses how wondrous
My journey shall prove.

4 Great spoils I shall win
From death, hell, and sin,
  'Midst outward afflictions
Shall feel Christ within;
And when I'm to die,
" Receive me!" I'll cry,
  For Jesus hath loved me,
I cannot tell why.

5 But this I do find:
We two are so joined,
  He'll not live in glory
And leave me behind;
So this is the race
I'm running through grace,
  Henceforth till admitted
To see my Lord's face.

6 And now I'm in care
My neighbors may share
  These blessings: to seek them
Will none of you dare?
In bondage, O why,
And death will you die,
  When one here assures you
Free grace is so nigh?

307   Fill Me Now.

1 Hover o'er me, Holy Spirit;
  Bathe my trembling heart and **brow;**
Fill me with thy hallowed presence,
  Come, O come and fill me now.

Chorus.

Fill me now, fill me now,
    Jesus, come and fill me now;
Fill me with thy hallowed presence,
    Come, O come and fill me now.

2 Thou canst fill me, gracious Spirit,
    Though I cannot tell thee how;
But I need thee, greatly need thee,
    Come, O come and fill me now.

3 I am weakness, full of weakness;
    At thy sacred feet I bow;
Blest, divine, eternal Spirit,
    Fill with power, and fill me now.

4 Cleanse and comfort, bless and save **me**;
    Bathe, O bathe my heart and brow!
Thou art comforting and saving,
    Thou art sweetly filling now.
Rev. E. H. Stokes, D.D.

308   I'M HAPPY.

1 I'M happy, I'm happy,
    O wondrous account!
My joys are immortal;
    I stand on the mount!
I gaze on my treasure,
    And long to be there,
With Jesus and angels,
    My kindred so dear.

2 O who is like Jesus?
    He's Salem's bright King!
He smiles and he loves me,
    And helps me to sing;

I'll praise him, I'll praise him,
  Whatever his will,
While rivers of pleasure
  My spirit doth fill.

3 I find him in singing,
  I find him in prayer;
In sweet meditation
  He always is there;
My constant companion,
  O may we ne'er part!
All glory to Jesus!
  He dwells in my heart.

309 A Charge to Keep I Have.

1 A CHARGE to keep I have,
  A God to glorify,
A never-dying soul to save,
  And fit it for the sky.

2 To serve the present age,
  My calling to fulfill,
O may it all my powers engage,
  To do my Master's will!

3 Arm me with jealous care,
  As in thy sight to live;
And O thy servant, Lord, prepare,
  A strict account to give.

4 Help me to watch and pray,
  And on thyself rely,
Assured, if I my trust betray,
  I shall forever die.

Charles Wesley.

310 My Soul, Be on Thy Guard.

1 My soul be on thy guard:
   Ten thousand foes arise;
The hosts of sin are pressing hard
   To draw thee from the skies.

2 O watch and fight and pray,
   The battle ne'er give o'er;
Renew it boldly ev'ry day,
   And help divine implore.

3 Ne'er think the vict'ry won,
   Nor lay thine armor down;
The work of faith will not be done
   Till thou obtain the crown.

4 Fight on, my soul, till death
   Shall bring thee to thy God;
He'll take thee, at thy parting breath,
   To his divine abode.

G. Heath.

311 Equip Me for the War.

1 Equip me for the war,
   And teach my hands to fight;
My simple, upright heart prepare,
   And guide my words aright.

2 Control my ev'ry thought,
   My whole of sin remove;
Let all my works in thee be wrought,
   Let all be wrought in love.

3 O arm me with the mind,
   Meek Lamb, that was in thee;
And let my knowing zeal be joined
   With perfect charity.

4 With calm and tempered zeal
   Let me enforce thy call;
And vindicate thy gracious will,
   Which offers life to all.

Charles Wesley.

312 LORD, IN THE STRENGTH OF GRACE.

1 LORD, in the strength of grace,
   With a glad heart and free,
Myself, my residue of days,
   I consecrate to thee.

2 Thy ransomed servant, I
   Restore to thee thine own;
And from this moment live or die,
   To serve my God alone.

Charles Wesley.

313   O LORD, HAVE MERCY.

1 THERE is a fountain filled with blood,
   Drawn from Immanuel's veins,
And sinners, plunged beneath that flood,
   Lose all their guilty stains.

Chorus.

O Lord have mercy, O Lord have mercy,
O Lord have mercy, have mercy on me.

2 The dying thief rejoiced to see
   That fountain in his day,
And there may I, though vile as he,
   Wash all my sins away.

3 Thou dying Lamb, thy precious blood
   Shall never lose its power
Till all the ransomed Church of God
   Are saved to sin no more.

4 E'er since by faith I saw the stream
  Thy flowing wounds supply,
Redeeming love has been my theme,
  And shall be till I die.
William Cowper.

314

ALAS! AND DID MY SAVIOUR BLEED?

1 ALAS! and did my Saviour bleed?
  And did my Sovereign die?
Would he devote that sacred head
  For such a worm as I?

2 Was it for crimes that I have done,
  He groaned upon the tree?
Amazing pity! grace unknown!
  And love beyond degree!

3 Well might the sun in darkness hide,
  And shut his glories in,
When Christ, the mighty Maker, died,
  For man, the creature's sin.

4 Thus might I hide my blushing face
  While his dear cross appears;
Dissolve my heart in thankfulness,
  And melt mine eyes to tears.

5 But drops of grief can ne'er repay
  The debt of love I owe;
Here, Lord, I give myself away—
  'Tis all that I can do.
Isaac Watts.

315 Lord, I Believe a Rest Remains.

1 Lord, I believes a rest remains
  To all thy people known;
A rest where pure enjoyment reigns,
  And thou art loved alone.

2 A rest where all our soul's desire
  Is fixed on things above;
Where fear and sin and grief expire,
  Cast out by perfect love.

5 O that I now the rest might know,
  Believe, and enter in;
Now, Saviour, now the power bestow,
  And let me cease from sin.

4 Remove this hardness from my heart;
  This unbelief remove;
To me the rest of faith impart,
  The Sabbath of thy love.
                              Charles Wesley.

316 I Can, I Will, I Do Believe.

I can, I will, I do believe,
I can, I will, I do believe.
I can, I will, I do believe
  That Jesus saves me now.

317 How I Love Jesus.

1 Alas! and did my Saviour bleed?
  And did my Sovereign die?
Would he devote that sacred head
  For such a worm as I?

Chorus.

O how I love Jesus,
O how I love Jesus,
O how I love Jesus,
Because he first loved me!

318 ROCK OF AGES.

1 Rock of Ages, cleft for me,
Let me hide myself in thee;
Let the water and the blood,
From thy wounded side which flowed,
Be of sin the double cure,
Save from wrath and make me pure.

2 Could my tears forever flow,
Could my zeal no languor know,
These for sin could not atone;
Thou must save, and thou alone:
In my hand no price I bring;
Simply to thy cross I cling.

3 While I draw this fleeting breath,
When my eyes shall close in death,
When I rise to worlds unknown,
And behold thee on thy throne,
Rock of Ages, cleft for me,
Let me hide myself in thee.

Toplady.

319 WHITER THAN SNOW.

1 DEAR Jesus, I long to be perfectly whole;
I want thee forever to live in my soul;
Break down ev'ry idol, cast out ev'ry foe;
Now wash me, and I shall be whiter
than snow.

2 Dear Jesus, let nothing unholy remain;
  Apply thine own blood, and extract
    ev'ry stain;
  To have this blessed washing, I all
    things forego,
  Now wash me, and I shall be whiter
    than snow.

3 Dear Jesus, come down from thy throne
    in the skies,
  And help me to make a complete sacri-
    fice;
  I give up myself, and whatever I know,
  Now wash me, and I shall be whiter
    than snow.

4 Dear Jesus, thou seest I patiently wait;
  Come now, and within me a new heart
    create;
  To those who have sought thee thou
    never said'st no,
  Now wash me, and I shall be whiter
    than snow.

5 Dear Jesus, for this I most humbly en-
    treat;
  I wait, blessèd Lord, at thy crucified feet;
  By faith, for my cleansing, I see thy
    blood flow;
  Now wash me, and I shall be whiter
    than snow.

6 The blessing by faith I receive from
    above;
  O glory! my soul is made perfect in love.
  My prayer has prevailed, and this mo-
    ment I know
  The blood is applied: I am whiter than
    snow.

315

320   WHAT A FRIEND?

1 WHAT a friend we have in Jesus,
    All our sins and griefs to bear!
What a privilege to carry
    Ev'ry thing to God in prayer!
O what peace we often forfeit,
    O what needless pains we bear,
All because we do not carry
    Every thing to God in prayer!

2 Have we trials and temptations?
    Is there trouble anywhere?
We should never be discouraged,
    Take it to the Lord in prayer.
Can we find a friend so faithful,
    Who will all our sorrows share?
Jesus knows our ev'ry weakness,
    Take it to the Lord in prayer,

3 Are we weak and heavy laden,
    Cumbered with a load of care?
Precious Saviour, still our refuge,
    Take it to the Lord in prayer.
Do thy friends despise, forsake thee?
    Take it to the Lord in prayer.
In his arms he'll take and shield thee,
    Thou wilt find a solace there.

321

LORD, I CARE NOT FOR RICHES.

1 LORD, I care not for riches,
    Neither silver nor gold;
I would make sure of heaven,
    I would enter the fold:

In the book of thy kingdom,
  With its pages so fair,
Tell me, Jesus my Saviour,
  Is my name written there?

Chorus.

Is my name written there,
On the page white and fair?
In the book of thy kingdom,
Is my name written there?

2 Lord, my sins they are many,
    Like the sands of the sea;
  But thy blood, O my Saviour,
    Is sufficient for me;
  For thy promise is written
    In bright letters that glow:
" Though your sins be as scarlet,
    I will make them like snow."

3 O that a beautiful city,
    With its mansions of light,
  With its glorified beings,
    In pure garments of white;
  Where no evil thing cometh
    To despoil what is fair,
  Where the angels are watching,
    Is my name written there?

322
WORK, FOR THE NIGHT IS COMING.

1 WORK, for the night is coming;
    Work through the morning hours;
  Work, while the dew is sparkling;
    Work 'mid springing flowers;

Work, when the day grows brighter;
  Work, in the glowing sun;
Work, for the night is coming,
  When man's work is done.

2 Work, for the night is coming;
  Work through the sunny noon;
Fill brightest hours with labor;
  Rest comes sure and soon.
Give every flying minute
  Something to keep in store;
Work, for the night is coming,
  When man works no more.

323   O Think of the Home.

1 O think of the home over there,
  By the side of the river of life,
Where the saints all immortal and fair,
  Are robed in their garments of white.

Chorus.

Over there, over there,
O think of a home over there!
Over there, over there,
O think of the home over there.

2 O think of the friends over there,
  Who before us the journey have trod,
Of the songs that they breathe on the air,
  In their home in the palace of God.

Chorus.

Over there, over there,
O think of the friends over there!
Over there, over there!
O think of the friends over there.

3 My Saviour is now over there,
 There my kindred and friends are at
  rest;
Then away from my sorrow and care,
 Let me fly to the land of the blest.

Chorus.

Over there, over there,
My Saviour is now over there!
Over there, over there,
My Saviour is now over there!

4 I'll soon be at home over there,
 For the end of my journey I see;
Many dear to my heart, over there,
 Are watching and waiting for me.

Chorus.

Over there, over there,
I'll soon be at home over there!
Over there, over there,
I'll soon be at home over there!

324
MORE LOVE TO THEE, O CHRIST.

1 MORE love to thee, O Christ,
 More love to thee!
Hear thou the prayer I make,
 On bended knee;
This is my earnest plea,
More love. O Christ, to thee,
 More love to thee!

2 Once earthly joy I craved,
 Sought peace and rest;
Now thee alone I seek,
 Give what is best:

This all my prayer shall be,
More love, O Christ, to thee,
More love to thee!

3 Then shall my latest breath
Whisper thy praise;
This be the parting cry
My heart shall raise,
This still its prayer shall be:
More love, O Christ, to thee,
More love to thee!

325   O for a Closer Walk!

1 O FOR a closer walk with God,
A calm and heav'nly frame;
A light to shine upon the road
That leads me to the Lamb!

2 Where is the blessèdness I knew,
When first I saw the Lord?
Where is the soul-refreshing view
Of Jesus and his word?

3 What peaceful hours I once enjoyed!
How sweet their mem'ry still!
But they have left an aching void
The world can never fill.

4 Return, O holy Dove, return;
Sweet messenger of rest!
I hate the sins that made thee **mourn,**
And drove thee from my breast.

5 The dearest idol I have known,
Whate'er that idol be,
Help me to tear it from thy **throne,**
And worship only thee.

6 So shall my walk be close with God
    Calm and serene my frame;
So purer light shall mark the road
    That leads me to the Lamb.

William Cowper.

326

MY FATHER IS RICH IN HOUSES AND LANDS.

1 My Father is rich in houses and lands,
    He holdeth the wealth of the world in
      his hands!
    Of rubies and diamonds, of silver and
      gold
    His coffers are full, he has riches untold.

Chorus.

    I'm the child of a King,
    The child of King;
      With Jesus my Saviour
    I'm the child of a King.

2 My father's own Son, the Saviour of
    men;
    Once wandered o'er earth as the poorest
      of them,
    But now he is reigning forever on high,
    And will give me a home in heav'n by
      and by.

3 I once was an outcast stranger on earth,
    A sinner by choice, an alien by birth!
    But I've been adopted, my name's
      written down,
    An heir to a mansion, a robe, and a
      crown.

21   321

4 A tent or a cottage, why should I care?
  They're building a palace for me over
    there!
  Though exiled from home, yet still I
    may sing:
  All glory to God, I'm the child of a King.

327 How Sweet the Name.

1 How sweet the name of Jesus sounds
    In a believer's ear!
  It soothes his sorrows, heals his wounds,
    And drives away his fear.

2 It makes the wounded spirit whole,
    And calms the troubled breast;
  'Tis manna to the hungry soul,
    And to the weary, rest.

3 Dear name! the rock on which I build,
    My shield and hiding-place;
  My never-failing treasure, filled
    With boundless stores of grace!

4 Jesus, my Shepherd, Saviour, Friend,
    My Prophet. Priest, and King,
  My Lord, my Life, my Way, my End,
    Accept the praise I bring!

5 I would thy boundless love proclaim
    With ev'ry fleeting breath;
  So shall the music of thy name
    Refresh my soul in death.
                    John Newton.

328   Am I a Soldier?

1 Am I a soldier of the cross,
    A foll'wer of the Lamb,
And shall I fear to own his cause,
    Or blush to speak his name?

2 Must I be carried to the skies
    On flow'ry beds of ease,
While others fought to win the prize,
    And sailed through bloody seas?

3 Are there no foes for me to face?
    Must I not stem the flood?
Is this vile world a friend to grace,
    To help me on to God?

4 Sure I must fight, if I would reign;
    Increase my courage, Lord;
I'll bear the toil, endure the pain,
    Supported by thy word.

5 Thy saints in all this glorious war
    Shall conquer, though they die;
They see the triumph from afar,
    By faith they bring it nigh.

6 When that illustrious day shall rise,
    And all thy armies shine
In robes of vict'ry through the skies,
    The glory shall be thine.
               Isaac Watts.

329   O Bliss of the Purified.

1 O bliss of the purified, bliss of the free,
    I plunge in the crimson tide open for
      me;

O'er sin and uncleanness exalting I
  stand,
And point to the print of the nails in
  his hand.

Chorus.

O sing of his mighty love,
  Sing of his mighty love,
  Sing of his mighty love,
    Mighty to save.

2 O bliss of the purified, Jesus is mine,
  No longer in dread condemnation I pine;
  In conscious salvation I sing of his grace,
  Who lifteth upon me the light of his face.

3 O bliss of the purified, bliss of the pure,
  No wound hath his soul that his blood
    cannot cure
  No sorrow-bowed head but may sweetly
    find rest,
  No tears but may dry them on Jesus'
    breast.

4 O Jesus the Crucified, thee will I sing,
  My blessèd Redeemer, my God, and my
    King;
  My soul filled with rapture shall shout
    o'er the grave,
  And triumph in death in the " Mighty
    to Save."

330

WHEN I CAN READ MY TITLE.

1 WHEN I can read my title clear
    To mansions in the skies,
  I bid farewell to ev'ry fear,
    And wipe my weeping eyes.

2 Should earth against my soul engage,
 And fiery darts be hurled,
Then I can smile at Satan's rage,
 And face a frowning world.

3 Let cares like a wild deluge come,
 Let storms of sorrow fall,
So I but safely reach my home,
 My God, my heav'n, my all.

4 There I shall bathe my weary soul
 In seas of heav'nly rest,
And not a wave of trouble roll
 Across my peaceful breast.

Isaac Watts.

331   I'll Live For Him.

1 My life, my love I give to thee,
 Thou Lamb of God, who died for me;
O may I ever faithful be,
 My Saviour and my God!

Chorus.

I'll live for him who died for me,
 How happy then my life shall be!
I'll live for him who died for me,
 My Saviour and my God!

2 I now believe thou dost receive,
 For thou hast died that I might live;
And now henceforth I'll trust in thee,
 My Saviour and my God!

3 O thou who died on Calvary,
 To save my soul and make me free,
I consecrate my life to thee,
 My Saviour and my God!

332 He Is Calling.

1 There's a wideness in God's mercy,
  Like the wideness of the sea;
There's a kindness in his justice
  Which is more than liberty.

Chorus.

He is calling: "Come to me!"
Lord, I'll gladly haste to thee.

2 There is a welcome for the sinner,
  And more graces for the good;
There is mercy with the Saviour;
  There is healing in his blood.

3 For the love of God is broader
  Than the measure of man's mind;
And the heart of the Eternal
  Is most wonderful and kind.

4 If our love were but more simple,
  We would take him at his word;
And our lives would be all sunshine
  In the sweetness of our Lord.
                                    Faber.

333
O That My Load.   L. M.

1 O that my load of sin were gone!
  O that I could at last submit
At Jesus' feet to lay it down—
  To lay my soul at Jesus' feet!

2 Rest for my soul I long to find:
  Saviour of all, if mine thou art,
Give me thy meek and lowly mind,
  And stamp thine image on my heart.

3 Break off the yoke of inbred sin,
    And fully set my spirit free;
I cannot rest till pure within,
    Till I am wholly lost in thee.

4 Fain would I learn of thee, my God,
    Thy light and easy burden prove,
The cross all stained with hallowed
      blood,
    The labor of thy dying love.

5 I would, but thou must give the pow'r;
    My heart from ev'ry sin release;
Bring near, bring near the joyful hour,
    And fill me with thy perfect peace.
                Charles Wesley.

334   I WILL SPRINKLE.

1 YE who know your sins forgiven,
    And are happy in the Lord,
Have you read that gracious promise
    Which is left upon record?

Refrain.

  I will sprinkle you with water,
    I will cleanse you from all sin,
Sanctify and make you holy,
    I will come and dwell within.

2 Though you have much peace and com-
      fort,
    Greater things you yet may find—
Freedom from unholy tempers,
    Freedom from the carnal mind.

3 Be as holy, and as happy,
    And as useful here below,

As it is your Father's pleasure;
Jesus, only Jesus know.

4 Spread, O spread the joyful tidings,
  Tell, O tell what God has done,
Till the nations are conformed
  To the image of his Son,

5 O may every soul be filled
  With the Holy Ghost to-day!
He is coming, he is coming;
  O prepare, prepare the way!

335 Sweet Land of Rest.

1 Sweet land of rest, for thee I sigh!
  When will the moment come,
When I shall lay my armor by,
  And dwell with Christ at home,
And dwell with Christ at home,
And dwell with Christ at home.

2 No tranquil joys on earth I know,
  No peaceful shelt'ring dome;
This world's a wilderness of woe,
  This world is not my home,
This world is not my home,
This world is not my home.

3 To Jesus Christ I sought for rest,
  He bade me cease to roam;
But fly for succor to his breast,
  And he'd conduct me home.
And he'd conduct me home,
And he'd conduct me home.

4 Weary of wand'ring round and round
   This vale of sin and gloom,
 I long to leave th' unhallowed ground
   And dwell with Christ at home,
 And dwell with Christ at home,
 And dwell with Christ at home.

336   Only Trust Him.

1 COME, ev'ry soul by sin oppressed,
   There's mercy with the Lord,
 And he will surely give you rest,
   By trusting in his word.

Chorus.

    Only trust him, only trust him,
      Only trust him now;
    He will save you, he will save you,
      He will save you now.

2 For Jesus shed his precious blood
   Rich blessings to bestow;
 Plunge now into the crimson flood,
   That washes white as snow.

3 Yes, Jesus is the Truth, the Way,
   That leads you into rest;
 Believe in him without delay,
   And you are fully blest.

4 Come then, and join this holy band,
   And on to glory go,
 To dwell in that celestial land,
   Where joys immortal flow.

Chorus.

Come to Jesus, come to Jesus,
  Come to Jesus now;
He will save you, he will save you,
  He will save you now.
        Rev. J. H. Stockton.

337   THE GREAT PHYSICIAN.

1 THE Great Physician now is here,
    The sympathizing Jesus;
  He speaks the drooping heart to cheer,
    O hear.the voice of Jesus.

Chorus.

Sweetest note in seraph song,
Sweetest name on mortal tongue,
Sweetest carol ever sung,
    Jesus, blessèd Jesus.

2 Your many sins are all forgiv'n,
    O hear the voice of Jesus;
  Go on your way in peace to heav'n
    And wear a crown with Jesus.

3 All glory to the dying Lamb!
    I now believe in Jesus;
  I love the blessèd Saviour's name,
    ·I love the name of Jesus.

4 The children, too, both great and small,
    Who love the name of Jesus,
  May now accept his gracious call
    To work and live for Jesus.

5 Come, brethren, help me sing his praise,
    O praise the name of Jesus;

Come, sisters, all your voices raise,
O bless the name of Jesus.

6 His name dispels my guilt and fear,
No other name but Jesus;
O how my soul delights to hear
The precious name of Jesus.

7 And when to that bright world above,
We rise to see our Jesus,
We'll sing around the throne of love
His name, the name of Jesus.

Rev. William H. Hunter, D.D.

338 It Is Good to Be Here.

1 WHILE we bow in thy name,
O meet us again,
Fill our hearts with the light of thy
love,
May the Spirit of grace,
And the smiles of thy grace,
Gently fall on us now from above!

Refrain.

It is good to be here, it is good to be
here,
Thy perfect love now drives away all
our fear,
And light streaming down makes the
pathway all clear,
It is good for us, Lord, to be here.

2 Our souls long for thee,
O may we now see
A sin-cleansing blood-wave appear;

And feel, as it rolls,
In power o'er our souls,
    It is good for us, Lord, to be here.

3 Thou art with us we know;
    We feel the sweet flow
        Of the sin-cleansing wave's gladd'ning
        tide;
    We are washed from our sin,
    Made all holy within,
        And in Jesus sweetly abide.

                        Rev. I. N. Wilson.

339   O How Happy Are They.

1 O now happy are they
    Who the Saviour obey,
        And have laid up their treasures above;
    Tongue can never express
    The sweet comfort and peace
        Of a soul in its earliest love.

2 That sweet comfort was mine,
    When the favor divine
        I received through the blood of the
        Lamb;
    When my heart first believed,
    What a joy I received—
        What a heaven in Jesus' name!

3 'Twas a heaven below
    My Redeemer to know,
        And the angels could do nothing
        more
    Than to fall at his feet,
    And the story repeat,
        And the Lover of sinners adore.

4 Jesus, all the day long,
   Was my joy and my song;
      O that all his salvation might see!
   He hath loved me, I cried,
   He hath suffered and died,
      To redeem even rebels like me.

340   TAKE ME AS I AM.

1 JESUS, my Lord, to thee I cry
   Unless thou help me I must die;
   O bring thy free salvation nigh,
      And take me as I am!

Refrain.

   Take me as I am,
   Take me as I am;
   O bring thy free salvation nigh,
      And take me as I am!

2 Helpless I am, and full of guilt,
   But yet for me thy blood was spilt,
   And thou can'st make me what thou
      wilt,
      But take me as I am!

3 I thirst, I long to know thy love,
   Thy full salvation I would prove;
   But since to thee I cannot move,
      O take me as I am!

4 If thou hast work for me to do,
   Inspire my will, my heart renew,
   And work both in and by me too,
      But take me as I am!

5 And when at last the work is done,
 The battle o'er, the vict'ry won,
 Still, still my cry shall be alone:
  "O take me as I am!"

Anon.

341   JUST AS I AM.

1 JUST as I am, without one plea,
 But that thy blood was shed for me,
 And that thou bidd'st me come to thee,
  O Lamb of God, I come!

2 Just as I am, and waiting not
 To rid my soul of one dark blot,
 To thee, whose blood can cleanse each
  spot,
  O Lamb of God, I come!

3 Just as I am, though tossed about
 With many a conflict, many a doubt,
 Fightings within and fears without,
  O Lamb of God, I come!

4 Just as I am—poor, wretched, blind—
 Sight, riches, healing of the mind;
 Yea, all I need in thee to find,
  O Lamb of God, I come!

5 Just as I am—thou wilt receive,
 Wilt welcome, pardon, cleanse, relieve;
 Because thy promise I believe,
  O Lamb of God, I come!

6 Just as I am—thy love unknown
 Hath broken every barrier down,
 Now, to be thine, yea, thine alone,
  O Lamb of God, I come!

342   More Faith in Jesus.

1 While struggling through this vale of
    tears
    I want more faith in Jesus;
Amid temptations, cares, and fears
    I want more faith in Jesus.

Chorus.

I want more faith, I want more faith,
    A clearer, brighter, stronger faith in
      Jesus;
And this my cry as time rolls by,
    I want more faith in Jesus.

2 To war against the foes within,
    I want more faith in Jesus;
To rise above the pow'rs of sin,
    I want more faith in Jesus.

3 To brave the storms that here I meet,
    I want more faith in Jesus;
To rest confiding at his feet,
    I want more faith in Jesus.

4 I want a faith that works by love,
    A constant faith in Jesus;
A faith that mountains can remove:
    A living faith in Jesus.
Henrietta E. Blair.

343   Hallelujah! Amen.

1 How oft in holy converse
    With Christ, my Lord, alone,
I seem to hear the millions
    That sing around his throne.

Chorus.

Hallelujah! Amen.
Hallelujah! Amen.
Hallelujah! Amen.
Amen, Amen.

2 They passed through toils and trials,
    And though the strife was long,
They share the victor's conquest,
    And sing the victor's song.

3 My soul takes up the chorus,
    And pressing on my way,
Communing still with Jesus,
    I sing from day to day.

4 Through grace I soon shall conquer,
    And reach my home on high,
And through eternal ages
    I'll shout beyond the sky.
                    Henrietta E. Blair.

344   O Thou in Whose.

1 O thou in whose presence my soul takes
    delight,
    On whom in affliction I call;
My comfort by day and my song in the
    night,
    My hope, my salvation, my all!

2 Where dost thou, dear Shepherd, resort
    with thy sheep
    To feed them in pastures of love?
Say, why in the valley of death should
    I weep,
    Or alone in this wilderness rove?

3 Or why should I wander an alien from
    thee,
  Or cry in the desert for bread?
Thy foes will rejoice when my sorrows
    they see,
  And smile at the tears I have shed.

4 Ye daughters of Zion, declare, have you
    seen
  The star that on Israel shone?
Say if in your tents my Beloved has
    been,
  And where with his flocks he has
  gone.

5 He looks! and ten thousands of angels
    rejoice,
  And myriads wait for his word;
He speaks! and eternity, filled with his
    voice,
  Re-echoes the praise of the Lord.

6 Dear Shepherd, I hear, and will follov
    thy call;
  I know the sweet sound of thy voice,
Restore and defend me, for thou art my
    all,
  And in thee I will ever rejoice.
Joseph Swain.

345   SESSIONS. L. M.

PRAISE God, from whom all blessings flow;
Praise him, all creatures here below;
Praise him above, ye heav'nly host
Praise Father, Son, and Holy Ghost

346 OLD HUNDRED. L. M.

PRAISE God, from whom all blessings flow ;
Praise him, all creatures here below ;
Praise him above, ye heav'nly host ;
Praise Father, Son, and Holy Ghost.

347 GLORIA PATRI.

1 GLORY to the Father and to the Son and
to the Holy Ghost ;
2 As it was in the beginning, is now, and
ever shall be, world without end.
Amen.

348 HE FULLY SAVES ME NOW.

1 I CAME to Jesus with my sin,
He fully saves me now ;
He washed away its ev'ry stain,
He fully saves me now.

Chorus.

He fully saves me now,
He freely saves me now ;
He washed away sin's every stain,
He fully saves me now.

2 Once guilty fears oppressed my soul,
He fully saves me now ;
His cleansing blood has made me whole,
He fully saves me now.

3 Sin's iron chains once held me fast,
He fully saves me now ;
But I'm redeemed, I'm free at last,
He fully saves me now.

4 Once all was dark, but now there's light,
  He fully saves me now ;
He found me blind, he gave me sight,
  He fully saves me now.

5 The Sun of Righteousness has risen,
  He fully saves me now ;
His beams have turned my hell to heaven,
  He fully saves me now.

6 Converted first at Calvary's cross,
  He fully saves me now ;
My barque on many a wave was tossed,
  He fully saves me now.

7 I sought again my Saviour's side,
  He fully saves me now ;
In the upper room was sanctified,
  He fully saves me now.

8 His gracious Spirit dwells within,
  He fully saves me now ;
His fire consumed indwelling sin,
  He fully saves me now.
                              Rev. L. L. Pickett.

349 LIFE'S RAILWAY TO HEAVEN.

1 LIFE is like a mountain railroad,
  With an engineer that's brave ;
We must make the run successful,
  From the cradle to the grave ;
Watch the curves, the fills, the tunnels,
  Never falter, never quail ;
Keep your hand upon the throttle,
  And your eye upon the rail.

Chorus.

Blessed Saviour, thou wilt guide us
  Till we reach that blissful shore ;

Where the angels wait to join us
In thy praise for evermore.

2 You will roll up grades of trial,
You will cross the bridge of strife ;
See that Christ is your conductor
On the lightning train of life ;
Always mindful of obstruction,
Do your duty, never fail ;
Keep your hand upon the throttle,
And your eye upon the rail.

3 You will always find obstructions,
Look for storms of wind and rain ;
On a fill, or curve, or trestle,
They will almost ditch your train ;
Put your trust alone in Jesus,
Never falter, never fail ;
Keep your hand upon the throttle,
And your eye upon the rail.

4 As you roll across the trestle,
Spanning death's dark swelling tide,
You behold the union depot,
Into which your train will glide ;
There you'll meet the Superintendent,
God the Father, God the Son,
With the hearty, joyous plaudit,
"Weary pilgrim, welcome home."
M. E. Abbey.

350 STEP OUT ON THE PROMISE.

1 O, MOURNER in Zion, how blessed art thou,
For Jesus is waiting to comfort thee now ;
Fear not to rely on the word of thy God;
Step out on the promise—get under the
blood.

2 O, ye that are hungry and thirsty, rejoice !
   For ye shall be filled ; do you hear that
      sweet voice
   Inviting you now to the banquet of God ?
   Step out on the promise—get under the
      blood.

3 Who sighs for a heart from iniquity free ?
   O, poor, troubled soul, there's a promise
      for thee !
   There's rest, weary one, in the bosom of
      God ;
   Step out on the promise—get under the
      blood.

4 Step out on the promise, and Christ you
      shall win ;
   " The blood of his Son cleanseth us from
      all sin ;"
   It cleanseth me now, hallelujah to God !
   I rest on his promise—I'm under the blood.
                  Maggie Potter.

351   My Happy Home.

1 Jerusalem, my happy home,
    Oh, how I long for thee !
  When will my sorrows have an end ?
    Thy joys, when shall I see ?

            Chorus.

  I will meet you in the city of the New
    Jerusalem,
    I am washed in the blood of the Lamb,
  I will meet you in the city of the New
    Jerusalem,
    I am washed in the blood of the Lamb.

2 Thy walls are all of precious stone,
  Most glorious to behold ;
Thy gates are richly set with pearl,
  Thy streets are paved with gold.

3 Thy gardens and thy pleasant streams
  My study long have been ;
Such sparkling gems by human sight
  Have never yet been seen.

4 Reach down, reach down thine arms of
    grace,
  And cause me to ascend,
Where congregations ne'er break up,
  And praises never end.

Anon.

352   KEEP CLOSE TO JESUS.

1 WHEN you start for the land of heavenly
    rest,
  Keep close to Jesus all the way ;
For he is the Guide and he knows the way
    best,
  Keep close to Jesus all the way.

Chorus.

Keep close to Jesus,
Keep close to Jesus,
Keep close to Jesus all the way ;
By day or by night never turn from the right,
Keep close to Jesus all the way.

2 Never mind the storms or trials as you go,
  Keep close to Jesus all the way ;
'Tis a comfort and joy his favor to know,
  Keep close to Jesus all the way.

342

3 To be safe from the darts of the evil one,
    Keep close to Jesus all the way ;
  Take the shield of faith till the victory is
      won,
    Keep close to Jesus all the way.

4 We shall reach our home in heaven by
      and by,
    Keep close to Jesus all the way ;
  Where to those we love we'll never say
      good-bye,
    Keep close to Jesus all the way.
                                    John Lane.

353 UNSEARCHABLE RICHES.

1 O THE unsearchable riches of Christ !—
    Wealth that can never be told ;—
  Riches exhaustless of mercy and grace,
    Precious, more precious than gold.

Chorus.

  Precious, more precious,—
    Wealth that can never be told ;
  O the unsearchable riches of Christ !
    Precious, more precious than gold.

2 O the unsearchable riches of Christ !
    Who shall their greatness declare ?
  Jewels whose lustre our lives may adorn,
    Pearls that the poorest may wear.

3 O the unsearchable riches of Christ !
    Freely, how freely they flow ;
  Making the souls of the faithful and true
    Happy wherever they go.

4 O the unsearchable riches of Christ !
  Who would not gladly endure
Trials, afflictions, and crosses on earth,
  Riches like those to secure ?

F. J. C.

354   Follow All the Way.

1 I have heard my Saviour calling,
  I have heard my Saviour calling,
  I have heard my Saviour calling,
" Take thy cross and follow, follow .

Chorus.

  Where he leads me I will follow,
  Where he leads me I will follow,
  Where he leads me I will follow,
I'll go with him, with him all the way.

2 Though he leads me through the valley,
  Though he leads me through the valley,
  Though he leads me through the valley,
I'll go with him, with him all the way.

3 Though he leads me through the garden,
  Though he leads me through the garden,
  Though he leads me through the garden,
I'll go with him, with him all the way.

4 Though the path be dark and dreary,
  Though the path be dark and dreary,
  Though the path be dark and dreary,
I'll go with him, with him all the way.

5 Though he leads me to the conflict,
  Though he leads me to the conflict,
  Though he leads me to the conflict,
I'll go with him, with him all the way.

344

6 Though he leads through fiery trials,
  Though he leads through fiery trials,
  Though he leads through fiery trials,
I'll go with him, with him all the way.

7 I will follow on to know him,
  I will follow on to know him,
  I will follow on to know him,
He's my Saviour, Saviour, Brother, Friend.

8 He will give me grace and glory,
  He will give me grace and glory,
  He will give me grace and glory,
He will keep me, keep me all the way.

9 O 'tis sweet to follow Jesus,
  O 'tis sweet to follow Jesus,
  O 'tis sweet to follow Jesus,
And be with him, with him all the way.

George W. Collins.

355   JESUS NOW IS CALLING.

1 COME, ye weary and oppressed,
    Jesus now is calling you;
  Come to him, he'll give you rest—
    Still he bids you come.

Refrain.

Jesus now is calling, calling, calling,
Jesus now is calling you—
Calling you to come.

2 Though your sins like mountains rise,
    Jesus now is calling you;
  He has made the sacrifice—
    Still he bids you come.

3 Though your sins like scarlet be,
    Jesus now is calling you;
  From your sins he'll set you free—
    Still he bids you come.

4 Come, ye wand'rers from the fold,
Jesus now is calling you ;
Oh, his love can ne'er be told !—
Still he bids you come.   *R. E. Hudson.*

356   THE VERY SAME JESUS.

1 COME, sinners, to the Living One,
He's just the same Jesus
As when he raised the widow's son,
The very same Jesus.

Chorus.
The very same Jesus,
The wonder working Jesus :
Oh, praise his name, he's just the same,
The very same Jesus.

2 Come, feast upon the "living bread,"
He's just the same Jesus
As when the multitudes he fed,
The very same Jesus.

3 Come, tell him all your griefs and fears,
He's just the same Jesus
As when he shed those loving tears,
The very same Jesus.

4 Come unto him for clearer light,
He's just the same Jesus
As when he gave the blind their sight,
The very same Jesus.

5 Calm 'midst the waves of trouble be,
He's just the same Jesus
As when he hushed the raging sea,
The very same Jesus.

6 Some day our raptured eyes shall see
He's just the same Jesus ;
Oh, blessed day for you and me !
The very same Jesus.
L. H. Edmunds.

INDEX.

SUPPLEMENT.

www.ingramcontent.com/pod-product-compliance
Lightning Source LLC
Chambersburg PA
CBHW030916270326
41929CB00008B/713